ESSAYS:

BY

R. W. EMERSON.

SECOND SERIES.

PHILADELPHIA:
DAVID McKAY, Publisher,
23 SOUTH NINTH STREET.
1889.

CONTENTS.

ESSAY I.

THE POET . . . . Page 5

ESSAY II.

EXPERIENCE 51

ESSAY III.

CHARACTER 97

ESSAY IV.

MANNERS 129

ESSAY V.

GIFTS 171

ESSAY VI.

NATURE 181

ESSAY VII.

POLITICS 213

ESSAY VIII.

NOMINALIST AND REALIST 241

NEW ENGLAND REFORMERS.

LECTURE AT AMORY HALL 269

(3)

THE POET.

A moody child and wildly wise
Pursued the game with joyful eyes,
Which chose, like meteors, their way,
And rived the dark with private ray:
They overleapt the horizon's edge,
Searched with Apollo's privilege;
Through man, and woman, and sea, and star,
Saw the dance of nature forward far;
Through worlds, and races, and terms, and times,
Saw musical order, and pairing rhymes.

(5)

Olympian bards who sung
   Divine ideas below,
Which always find us young,
   And always keep us so.

ESSAY I.

THE POET.

Those who are esteemed umpires of taste, are often persons who have acquired some knowledge of admired pictures or sculptures, and have an inclination for whatever is elegant; but if you inquire whether they are beautiful souls, and whether their own acts are like fair pictures, you learn that they are selfish and sensual. Their cultivation is local, as if you should rub a log of dry wood in one spot to produce fire, all the rest remaining cold. Their knowledge of the fine arts is some study of rules and particulars, or some limited judgment of color or form, which is exercised for amusement or for show. It is a proof of the shallowness of the doctrine of beauty, as it lies in the minds of our amateurs, that men seem to have lost the perception of the instant dependence of form upon soul. There is no doctrine of forms in our philosophy. We were put into our bodies, as

7

fire is put into a pan, to be carried about; but there is no accurate adjustment between the spirit and the organ, much less is the latter the germination of the former. So in regard to other forms, the intellectual men do not believe in any essential dependence of the material world on thought and volition. Theologians think it a pretty air-castle to talk of the spiritual meaning of a ship or a cloud, of a city or a contract, but they prefer to come again to the solid ground of historical evidence; and even the poets are contented with a civil and conformed manner of living, and to write poems from the fancy, at a safe distance from their own experience. But the highest minds of the world have never ceased to explore the double meaning, or, shall I say, the quadruple, or the centuple, or much more manifold meaning, of every sensuous fact: Orpheus, Empedocles, Heraclitus, Plato, Plutarch, Dante, Swedenborg, and the masters of sculpture, picture, and poetry. For we are not pans and barrows, nor even porters of the fire and torch-bearers, but children of the fire, made of it, and only the same divinity transmuted, and at two or three removes, when we know least about it. And this hidden truth, that the fountains whence all this river of Time, and its creatures, floweth, are intrinsically ideal and beautiful, draws us to the consideration of the nature and functions of the Poet, or the man of Beauty, to the means and materials he uses, and to the general aspect of the art in the present time.

The breadth of the problem is great, for the poet is representative. He stands among partial men for the complete man, and apprises us not of his wealth, but of the commonwealth. The young man reveres men of genius, because, to speak truly, they are more himself than he is. They receive of the soul as he also receives, but they more. Nature enhances her beauty, to the eye of loving men, from their belief that the poet is beholding her shows at the same time. He is isolated among his contemporaries, by truth and by his art, but with this consolation in his pursuits, that they will draw all men sooner or later. For all men live by truth, and stand in need of expression. In love, in art, in avarice, in politics, in labor, in games, we study to utter our painful secret. The man is only half himself, the other half is his expression.

Notwithstanding this necessity to be published,

adequate expression is rare. I know not how it is that we need an interpreter; but the great majority of men seen to be minors, who have not yet come into possession of their own, or mutes, who cannot report the conversation they have had with nature. There is no man who does not anticipate a supersensual utility in the sun, and stars, earth, and water. These stand and wait to render him a peculiar service. But there is some obstruction, or some excess of phlegm in our constitution, which does not suffer them to yield the due effect. Too feeble fall the impressions of nature on us to make us artists. Every touch should thrill. Every man should be so much an artist, that he could report in conversation what had befallen him. Yet, in our experience, the rays or appulses have sufficient force to arrive at the senses, but not enough to reach the quick, and compel the reproduction of themselves in speech. The poet is the person in whom these powers are in balance, the man without impediment, who sees and handles that which others dream of, traverses the whole scale of experience, and is representative of man, in virtue of being the largest power to receive and to impart.

For the Universe has three children, born at one time, which reappear, under different names, in every system of thought, whether they be called cause, operation, and effect; or, more poetically, Jove, Pluto, Neptune; or, theologically, the Father, the Spirit, and the Son; but which we will call here, the Knower, the Doer, and the Sayer. These stand respectively for the love of truth, for the love of good, and for the love of beauty. These three are equal. Each is that which he is essentially, so that he cannot be surmounted or analyzed, and each of these three has the power of the others latent in him, and his own patent.

The poet is the sayer, the namer, and represents beauty. He is a sovereign, and stands on the centre. For the world is not painted, or adorned, but is from the beginning beautiful; and God has not made some beautiful things, but Beauty is the creator of the universe. Therefore the poet is not any permissive potentate, but is emperor in his own right. Criticism is infested with a cant of materialism, which assumes that manual skill and activity is the first merit of all men, and disparages such as say and do not, overlooking the fact that some men, namely, poets, are natural sayers, sent into the world to the end of expression, and confounds them with those whose province is action, but who quit it to imitate the sayers. But Homer's words are as costly and admirable to Homer, as Agamemnon's victories are to Agamemnon. The poet does not wait for the hero or the sage, but, as they act and think primarily, so he writes primarily what will and must be spoken, reckoning the others, though primaries also, yet, in respect to him, secondaries and servants; as sitters or models in the studio of a painter, or as assistants who bring building materials to an architect.

For poetry was all written before time was, and whenever we are so finely organized that we can penetrate into that region where the air is music, we hear those primal warblings, and attempt to write them down, but we lose ever and anon a word, or a verse, and substitute something of our own, and thus miswrite the poem. The men of more delicate ear write down these cadences more faithfully, and these transcripts, though imperfect, become the songs of the nations. For nature is as truly beautiful as it is good, or as it is reasonable, and must as much appear, as it must be done, or be known. Words and deeds are quite indifferent modes of the divine energy. Words are also actions, and actions are a kind of words.

The sign and credentials of the poet are, that he announces that which no man foretold. He is the true and only doctor; he knows and tells; he is the only teller of news, for he was present and privy to the appearance which he describes. He is a beholder of ideas, and an utterer of the necessary and causal. For we do not speak now of men of poetical talents, or of industry and skill in metre, but of the true poet. I took part in a conversation the other day, concerning a recent writer of lyrics, a man of subtle mind, whose head appeared to be a music-box of delicate tunes and rhythms, and whose skill, and command of language, we could not sufficiently praise. But when the question arose, whether he was not only a lyrist, but a poet, we were obliged to confess that he is plainly a contemporary, not an eternal man. He does not stand out of our low limitations, like a Chimborazo under the line, running up from the torrid base through all the climates of the globe, with belts of the herbage of every latitude on its high and mottled sides; but this genius is the landscape-garden of a modern house, adorned with fountains and statues, with well-bred men and women standing and sitting in the walks and terraces. We hear, through all the varied music, the ground-tone of conventional life. Our poets are men of talents who sing, and not the children of music. The argument is secondary, the finish of the verses is primary.

For it is not metres, but a metre-making argument, that makes a poem,—a thought so passionate and alive, that, like the spirit of a plant or an animal, it has an architecture of its own, and adorns nature with a new thing. The thought and the form are equal in the order of time, but in the order of genesis the thought is prior to the form. The poet has a new thought: he has a whole new experience to unfold; he will tell us how it was with him, and all men will be the richer in his fortune. For, the experience of each new age requires a new confession, and the world seems always waiting for its poet. I remember, when I was young, how much I was moved one morning by tidings that genius had appeared in a youth who sat

near me at table. He had left his work, and
gone rambling none knew whither, and had
written hundreds of lines, but could not tell
whether that which was in him was therein
told: he could tell nothing but that all was
changed,—man, beast, heaven, earth, and sea.
How gladly we listened! how credulous!
Society seemed to be compromised. We sat in
the aurora of a sunrise which was to put out all
the stars. Boston seemed to be at twice the
distance it had the night before, or was much
farther than that. Rome,—what was Rome?
Plutarch and Shakspeare were in the yellow
leaf, and Homer no more should be heard of.
It is much to know that poetry has been written
this very day, under this very roof, by your
side. What! that wonderful spirit has not ex-
pired! these stony moments are still sparkling
and animated! I had fancied that the oracles
were all silent, and nature had spent her fires,
and behold! all night, from every pore, these
fine auroras have been streaming. Every one
has some interest in the advent of the poet, and
no one knows how much it may concern him.
We know that the secret of the world is profound, but who or what shall be our interpreter,

we know not. A mountain ramble, a new style of face, a new person, may put the key into our hands. Of course, the value of genius to us is in the veracity of its report. Talent may frolic and juggle; genius realizes and adds. Mankind, in good earnest, have availed so far in understanding themselves and their work, that the foremost watchman on the peak announces his news. It is the truest word ever spoken, and the phrase will be the fittest, most musical, and the unerring voice of the world for that time.

All that we call sacred history attests that the birth of a poet is the principal event in chronology. Man, never so often deceived, still watches for the arrival of a brother who can hold him steady to a truth, until he has made it his own. With what joy I begin to read a poem, which I confide in as an inspiration! And now my chains are to be broken; I shall mount above these clouds and opaque airs in which I live,—opaque, though they seem transparent,—and from the heaven of truth I shall see and comprehend my relations. That will reconcile me to life, and renovate nature, to see trifles animated by a tendency, and to know what I am doing. Life will no more be a noise; now I shall see men and women, and know the signs by which they may be discerned from fools and satans. This day shall be better than my birthday: then I became an animal: now I am invited into the science of the real. Such is the hope, but the fruition is postponed. Oftener it falls, that this winged man, who will carry me into the heaven, whirls me into the clouds, then leaps and frisks about with me from cloud to cloud, still affirming that he is bound heavenward; and I, being myself a novice, am slow in perceiving that he does not know the way into the heavens, and is merely bent that I should admire his skill to rise, like a fowl or a flying fish, a little way from the ground or the water; but the all-piercing, all-feeding, and ocular air of heaven, that man shall never inhabit. I tumble down again soon into my old nooks, and lead the life of exaggerations as before, and have lost my faith in the possibility of any guide who can lead me thither where I would be.

But leaving these victims of vanity, let us, with new hope, observe how nature, by worthier impulses, has ensured the poet's fidelity to his office of announcement and affirming,

27

namely, by the beauty of things, which becomes a new, and higher beauty, when expressed. Nature offers all her creatures to him as a picture-language. Being used as a type, a second wonderful value appears in the object, far better than its old value, as the carpenter's stretched cord, if you hold your ear close enough, is musical in the breeze. "Things more excellent than every image," says Jamblichus, "are expressed through images." Things admit of being used as symbols, because nature is a symbol, in the whole, and in every part. Every line we can draw in the sand, has expression; and there is no body without its spirit or genius. All form is an effect of character; all condition, of the quality of the life; all harmony, of health; (and, for this reason, a perception of beauty should be sympathetic, or proper only to the good.) The beautiful rests on the foundations of the necessary. The soul makes the body, as the wise Spenser teaches :—

> "So every spirit, as it is most pure,
> And hath in it the more of heavenly light,
> So it the fairer body doth procure
> To habit in, and it more fairly dight,
> With cheerful grace and amiable sight.
> For, of the soul, the body form doth take,
> For soul is form, and doth the body make."

Here we find ourselves, suddenly, not in a critical speculation, but in a holy place, and should go very warily and reverently. We stand before the secret of the world, there where Being passes into Appearance, and Unity into Variety.

The Universe is the externisation of the soul. Wherever the life is, that bursts into appearance around it. Our science is sensual, and therefore superficial. The earth, and the heavenly bodies, physics, and chemistry, we sensually treat, as if they were self-existent; but these are the retinue of that Being we have. " The mighty heaven," said Proclus, " exhibits, in its transfigurations, clear images of the splendor of intellectual perceptions; being moved in conjunction with the unapparent periods of intellectual natures." Therefore, science always goes abreast with the just elevation of the man, keeping step with religion and metaphysics; or, the state of science is an index of our self-knowledge. Since everything in nature answers to a moral power, if any phenomenon remains brute and dark, it is that the corresponding faculty in the observer is not yet active.

No wonder, then, if these waters be so deep, that we hover over them with a religious regard. The beauty of the fable proves the importance of the sense; to the poet, and to all others; or, if you please, every man is so far a poet as to be susceptible of these enchantments of nature : for all men have the thoughts whereof the universe is the celebration. I find that the fascination resides in the symbol. Who loves nature? Who does not? Is it only poets, and men of leisure and cultivation, who live with her? No; but also hunters, farmers, grooms, and butchers, though they express their affection in their choice of life, and not in their choice of words. The writer wonders what the coachman or the hunter values in riding, in horses, and dogs. It is not superficial qualities. When you talk with him, he holds these at as slight a rate as you. His worship is sympathetic; he has no definitions, but he is commanded in nature, by the living power which he feels to be there present. No imitation, or playing of these things, would content him; he loves the earnest of the north-wind, of rain, of stone, and wood, and iron. A beauty not explicable, is dearer than a beauty which we can see to the end of. It is nature the symbol, nature certifying the supernatural, body overflowed by life, which he worships, with coarse, but sincere rites.

The inwardness, and mystery, of this attachment, drives men of every class to the use of emblems. The schools of poets, and philosophers, are not more intoxicated with their symbols, than the populace with theirs. In our political parties, compute the power of badges and emblems. See the great ball which they roll from Baltimore to Bunker hill! In the political processions, Lowell goes in a loom, and Lynn in a shoe, and Salem in a ship. Witness the cider-barrel, the log-cabin, the hickory-stick, the palmetto, and all the cognizances of party. See the power of national emblems. Some stars, lilies, leopards, a crescent, a lion, an eagle, or other figure, which came into credit God knows how, on an old rag of bunting, blowing in the wind, on a fort, at the ends of the earth, shall make the blood tingle under the rudest, or the most conventional exterior. The people fancy they hate poetry, and they are all poets and mystics!

Beyond this universality of the symbolic language, we are apprised of the divineness of this superior use of things, whereby the world

is a temple, whose walls are covered with emblems, pictures, and commandments of the
Deity, in this, that there is no fact in nature
which does not carry the whole sense of nature;
and the distinctions which we make in events,
and in affairs, of low and high, honest and base,
disappear when nature is used as a symbol.
Thought makes everything fit for use. The
vocabulary of an omniscient man would embrace words and images excluded from polite
conversation. What would be base, or even
obscene, to the obscene, becomes illustrious,
spoken in a new connexion of thought. The
piety of the Hebrew prophets purges their
grossness. The circumcision is an example of
the power of poetry to raise the low and offensive. Small and mean things serve as well as
great symbols. The meaner the type by which
a law is expressed, the more pungent it is, and
the more lasting in the memories of men: just
as we choose the smallest box, or case, in which
any needful utensil can be carried. Bare lists
of words are found suggestive, to an imaginative and excited mind; as it is related of Lord
Chatham, that he was accustomed to read in
Bailey's Dictionary, when he was preparing to

speak in Parliament. The poorest experience is rich enough for all the purposes of expressing thought. Why covet a knowledge of new facts? Day and night, house and garden, a few books, a few actions, serve us as well as would all trades and all spectacles. We are far from having exhausted the significance of the few symbols we use. We can come to use them yet with a terrible simplicity. It does not need that a poem should be long. Every word was once a poem. Every new relation is a new word. Also, we use defects and deformities to a sacred purpose, so expressing our sense that the evils of the world are such only to the evil eye. In the old mythology, mythologists observe, defects are ascribed to divine natures, as lameness to Vulcan, blindness to Cupid, and the like, to signify exuberances.

For, as it is dislocation and detachment from the life of God, that makes things ugly, the poet, who re-attaches things to nature and the Whole,—re-attaching even artificial things, and violations of nature, to nature, by a deeper insight,—disposes very easily of the most disagreeable facts. Readers of poetry see the factory-village and the railway, and fancy that the poetry of the landscape is broken up by these; for these works of art are not yet consecrated in their reading; but the poet sees them fall within the great Order not less than the bee-hive, or the spider's geometrical web. Nature adopts them very fast into her vital circles, and the gliding train of cars she loves like her own. Besides, in a centred mind, it signifies nothing how many mechanical inventions you exhibit. Though you add millions, and never so surprising, the fact of mechanics has not gained a grain's weight. The spiritual fact remains unalterable, by many or by few particulars; as no mountain is of any appreciable height to break the curve of the sphere. A shrewd country-boy goes to the city for the first time, and the complacent citizen is not satisfied with his little wonder. It is not that he does not see all the fine houses, and know that he never saw such before, but he disposes of them as easily as the poet finds place for the railway. The chief value of the new fact, is to enhance the great and constant fact of Life, which can dwarf any and every circumstance, and to which the belt of wampum, and the commerce of America, are alike.

The world being thus put under the mind for
verb and noun, the poet is he who can articulate
it. For, though life is great, and fascinates,
and absorbs,—and though all men are intelligent of the symbols through which it is named,
—yet they cannot originally use them. We
are symbols, and inhabit symbols; workman,
work, and tools, words and things, birth and
death, all are emblems; but we sympathize with
the symbols, and, being infatuated with the
economical uses of things, we do not know that
they are thoughts. The poet, by an ulterior
intellectual perception, gives them a power
which makes their old use forgotten, and puts
eyes, and a tongue, into every dumb and in-
animate object. He perceives the independence
of the thought on the symbol, the stability of
the thought, the accidency and fugacity of the
symbol. As the eyes of Lyncæus were said to
see through the earth, so the poet turns the
world to glass, and shows us all things in their
right series and procession. For, through that
better perception, he stands one step nearer to
things, and sees the flowing or metamorphosis;
perceives that thought is multiform; that within
the form of every creature is a force impelling

it to ascend into a higher form; and, following with his eyes the life, uses the forms which express that life, and so his speech flows with the flowing of nature. All the facts of the animal economy, sex, nutriment, gestation, birth, growth, are symbols of the passage of the world into the soul of man, to suffer there a change, and reappear a new and higher fact. He uses forms according to the life, and not according to the form. This is true science. The poet alone knows astronomy, chemistry, vegetation, and animation, for he does not stop at these facts, but employs them as signs. He knows why the plain, or meadow of space, was strown with these flowers we call suns, and moons, and stars; why the great deep is adorned with animals, with men, and gods; for, in every word he speaks he rides on them as the horses of thought.

By virtue of this science the poet is the Namer, or Language-maker, naming things sometimes after their appearance, sometimes after their essence, and giving to every one its own name and not another's, thereby rejoicing the intellect, which delights in detachment or boundary. The poets made all the words, and therefore language is the archives of history, and, if we must say it, a sort of tomb of the muses. For, though the origin of most of our words is forgotten, each word was at first a stroke of genius, and obtained currency, because for the moment it symbolized the world to the first speaker and to the hearer. The etymologist finds the deadest word to have been once a brilliant picture. Language is fossil poetry. As the limestone of the continent consists of infinite masses of the shells of animalcules, so language is made up of images, or tropes, which now, in their secondary use, have long ceased to remind us of their poetic origin. But the poet names the thing because he sees it, or comes one step nearer to it than any other. This expression, or naming, is not art, but a second nature, grown out of the first, as a leaf out of a tree. What we call nature, is a certain self-regulated motion, or change; and nature does all things by her own hands, and does not leave another to baptise her, but baptises herself; and this through the metamorphosis again. I remember that a certain poet described it to me thus:

Genius is the activity which repairs the decays of things, whether wholly or partly of a material and finite kind. Nature, through all her kingdoms, insures herself. Nobody cares for planting the poor fungus: so she shakes down from the gills of one agaric countless spores, any one of which, being preserved, transmits new billions of spores to-morrow or next day. The new agaric of this hour has a chance which the old one had not. This atom of seed is thrown into a new place, not subject to the accidents which destroyed its parent two rods off. She makes a man; and having brought him to ripe age, she will no longer run the risk of losing this wonder at a blow, but she detaches from him a new self, that the kind may be safe from accidents to which the individual is exposed. So when the soul of the poet has come to ripeness of thought, she detaches and sends away from it its poems or songs,—a fearless, sleepless, deathless progeny, which is not exposed to the accidents of the weary kingdom of time: a fearless, vivacious offspring, clad with wings, (such was the virtue of the soul out of which they came), which carry them fast and far, and infix them irrecoverably

into the hearts of men. These wings are the
beauty of the poet s soul. The songs, thus
flying immortal from their mortal parent, are
pursued by clamorous flights of censures, which
swarm in far greater numbers, and threaten to
devour them; but these last are not winged.
At the end of a very short leap they fall plump
down, and rot, having received from the souls
out of which they came no beautiful wings.
But the melodies of the poet ascend, and leap,
and pierce into the deeps of infinite time.

So far the bard taught me, using his freer
speech. But nature has a higher end, in the pro-
duction of new individuals, than security, namely,
ascension, or, the passage of the soul into
higher forms. I knew, in my younger days, the
sculptor who made the statue of the youth
which stands in the public garden. He was,
as I remember, unable to tell, directly, what
made him happy, or unhappy, but by wonderful indirections he could tell. He rose one day,
according to his habit, before the dawn, and saw
the morning break, grand as the eternity out of
which it came, and, for many days after, he
strove to express this tranquillity, and, lo! his

chisel had fashioned out of marble the form of a beautiful youth, Phosphorus, whose aspect is such, that, it is said, all persons who look on it become silent. The poet also resigns himself to his mood, and that thought which agitated him is expressed, but *alter idem,* in a manner totally new. The expression is organic, or, the new type which things themselves take when liberated. As, in the sun, objects paint their images on the retina of the eye, so they, sharing the aspiration of the whole universe, tend to paint a far more delicate copy of their essence in his mind. Like the metamorphosis of things into higher organic forms, is their change into melodies. Over everything stands its dæmon, or soul, and, as the form of the thing is reflected by the eye, so the soul of the thing is reflected by a melody. The sea, the mountain-ridge, Niagara, and every flower-bed, pre-exist, or super-exist, in pre-cantations, which sail like odors in the air, and when any man goes by with an ear sufficiently fine, he overhears them, and endeavors to write down the notes, without diluting or depraving them. And herein is the legitimation of criticism, in the mind's faith, that the poems are a corrupt version of some text in nature, with which they ought to be made to tally. A rhyme in one of our sonnets should not be less pleasing than the iterated nodes of a sea-shell, or the resembling difference of a group of flowers. The pairing of the birds is an idyl, not tedious as our idyls are; a tempest is a rough ode without falsehood or rant; a summer, with its harvest sown, reaped, and stored, is an epic song, subordinating how many admirably executed parts. Why should not the symmetry and truth that modulate these, glide into our spirits, and we participate the invention of nature?

This insight, which expresses itself by what is called Imagination, is a very high sort of seeing, which does not come by study, but by the intellect being where and what it sees, by sharing the path, or circuit of things through forms, and so making them translucid to others. The path of things is silent. Will they suffer a speaker to go with them? A spy they will not suffer; a lover, a poet, is the transcendency of their own nature,—him they will suffer. The condition of true naming, on the poet's part, is his resigning himself to the divine *aura* which breathes through forms, and accompanying that.

It is a secret which every intellectual man quickly learns, that, beyond the energy of his possessed and conscious intellect, he is capable of a new energy (as of an intellect doubled on itself), by abandonment to the nature of things; that, besides his privacy of power as an individual man, there is a great public power, on which he can draw, by unlocking, at all risks, his human doors, and suffering the ethereal tides to roll and circulate through him : then he is caught up into the life of the Universe, his speech is thunder, his thought is law, and his words are universally intelligible as the plants and animals. The poet knows that he speaks adequately, then, only when he speaks somewhat wildly, or, " with the flower of the mind; " not with the intellect, used as an organ, but with the intellect released from all service, and suffered to take its direction from its celestial life ; or, as the ancients were wont to express themselves, not with intellect alone, but with the intellect inebriated by nectar. As the traveller who has lost his way, throws his reins on his horse's neck, and trusts to the instinct of the animal to find his road, so must we do with the divine animal who carries us through this

world. For if in any manner we can stimulate
this instinct, new passages are opened for us
into nature, the mind flows into and through
things hardest and highest, and the metamorphosis is possible.

This is the reason why bards love wine, mead,
narcotics, coffee, tea, opium, the fumes of
sandal-wood and tobacco, or whatever other
species of animal exhilaration. All men avail
themselves of such means as they can, to add
this extraordinary power to their normal powers ;
and to this end they prize conversation, music,
pictures, sculpture, dancing, theatres, travelling,
war, mobs, fires, gaming, politics, or love, or
science, or animal intoxication, which are several
coarser or finer *quasi*-mechanical substitutes for
the true nectar, which is the ravishment of the
intellect by coming nearer to the fact. These are
auxiliaries to the centrifugal tendency of a man,
to his passage out into free space, and they help
him to escape the custody of that body in which
he is pent up, and of that jail-yard of individual
relations in which he is enclosed. Hence a
great number of such as were professionally ex-
pressors of Beauty, as painters, poets, musicians,
and actors, have been more than others wont to

28

lead a life of pleasure and indulgence; all but
the few who received the true nectar; and, as
it was a spurious mode of attaining freedom, as
it was an emancipation not into the heavens,
but into the freedom of baser places, they were
punished for that advantage they won, by a
dissipation and deterioration.   But never can any
advantage be taken of nature by a trick.   The
spirit of the world, the great calm presence of
the creator, comes not forth to the sorceries of
opium or of wine.   The sublime vision comes
to the pure and simple soul in a clean and
chaste body.   That is not an inspiration which
we owe to narcotics, but some counterfeit excitement and fury.   Milton says, that the lyric
poet may drink wine and live generously, but
the epic poet, he who shall sing of the gods,
and their descent unto men, must drink water
out of a wooden bowl.   For poetry is not
' Devil's wine,' but God's wine.   It is with this
as it is with toys.   We fill the hands and nur-
series of our children with all manner of dolls,
drums, and horses, withdrawing their eyes from
the plain face and sufficing objects of nature,
the sun, and moon, the animals, the water, and
stones, which should be their toys.   So the

poet's habit of living should be set on a key so low and plain, that the common influences should delight him. His cheerfulness should be the gift of the sunlight; the air should suffice for his inspiration, and he should be tipsy with water. That spirit which suffices quiet hearts, which seems to come forth to such from every dry knoll of sere grass, from every pine-stump, and half-imbedded stone, on which the dull March sun shines, comes forth to the poor and hungry, and such as are of simple taste. If thou fill thy brain with Boston and New York, with fashion and covetousness, and wilt stimulate thy jaded senses with wine and French coffee, thou shalt find no radiance of wisdom in the lonely waste of the pinewoods.

If the imagination intoxicates the poet, it is not inactive in other men. The metamorphosis excites in the beholder an emotion of joy. The use of symbols has a certain power of emancipation and exhilaration for all men. We seem to be touched by a wand, which makes us dance and run about happily, like children. We are like persons who come out of a cave or cellar into the open air. This is the effect on us of tropes, fables, oracles, and all poetic forms.

Poets are thus liberating gods. Men have really got a new sense, and found within their world, another world, or nest of worlds; for, the metamorphosis once seen, we divine that it does not stop. I will not now consider how much this makes the charm of algebra and the mathematics, which also have their tropes, but it is felt in every definition; as, when Aristotle defines *space* to be an immovable vessel, in which things are contained;—or, when Plato defines a *line* to be a flowing point; or, *figure* to be a bound of solid; and many the like. What a joyful sense of freedom we have, when Vitruvius announces the old opinion of artists, that no architect can build any house well, who does not know something of anatomy. When Socrates, in Charmides, tells us that the soul is cured of its maladies by certain incantations, and that these incantations are beautiful reasons, from which temperance is generated in souls; when Plato calls the world an animal; and Timæus affirms that the plants also are animals; or affirms a man to be a heavenly tree, growing with his root, which is his head, upward; and, as George Chapman, following him, writes,—

> "So in our tree of man, whose nervie root
> Springs in his top;"

when Orpheus speaks of hoariness as "that white flower which marks extreme old age;" when Proclus calls the universe the statue of the intellect; when Chaucer, in his praise of 'Gentilesse,' compares good blood in mean condition to fire, which, though carried to the darkest house betwixt this and the mount of Caucasus, will yet hold its natural office, and burn as bright as if twenty thousand men did it behold; when John saw, in the apocalypse, the ruin of the world through evil, and the stars fall from heaven, as the figtree casteth her untimely fruit; when Æsop reports the whole catalogue of common daily relations through the masquerade of birds and beasts;—we take the cheerful hint of the immortality of our essence, and its versatile habit and escapes, as when the gypsies say, "it is in vain to hang them, they cannot die."

The poets are thus liberating gods. The ancient British bards had for the title of their order, "Those who are free throughout the world." They are free, and they make free. An imaginative book renders us much more service at first, by stimulating us through its tropes, than afterward, when we arrive at the precise sense of the author. I think nothing is of any value in books, excepting the transcendental and extraordinary. If a man is inflamed and carried away by his thought, to that degree that he forgets the authors and the public, and heeds only this one dream, which holds him like an insanity, let me read his paper, and you may have all the arguments and histories and criticism. All the value which attaches to Pythagoras, Paracelsus, Cornelius Agrippa, Cardan, Kepler, Swedenborg, Schelling, Oken, or any other who introduces questionable facts into his cosmogony, as angels, devils, magic, astrology, palmistry, mesmerism, and so on, is the certificate we have of departure from routine, and that here is a new witness. That also is the best success in conversation, the magic of liberty, which puts the world, like a ball, in our hands. How cheap even the liberty then seems; how mean to study, when an emotion communicates to the intellect the power to sap and upheave nature: how great the perspective! nations, times, systems, enter and disappear, like threads in tapestry of large figure and many colors; dream delivers us to dream, and, while the drunkenness lasts, we will sell our bed, our philosophy, our religion, in our opulence.

There is good reason why we should prize this liberation. The fate of the poor shepherd, who, blinded and lost in the snow-storm, perishes in a drift within a few feet of his cottage door, is an emblem of the state of man. On the brink of the waters of life and truth, we are miserably dying. The inaccessibleness of every thought but that we are in, is wonderful. What if you come near to it,—you are as remote, when you are nearest, as when you are farthest. Every thought is also a prison; every heaven is also a prison. Therefore we love the poet, the inventor, who in any form, whether in an ode, or in an action, or in looks and behavior, has yielded us a new thought. He unlocks our chains, and admits us to a new scene.

This emancipation is dear to all men, and the power to impart it, as it must come from greater depth and scope of thought, is a measure of intellect. Therefore all books of the imagination endure, all which ascend to that truth, that the writer sees nature beneath him, and uses it as his exponent. Every verse or sentence, possessing this virtue, will take care of its own immortality. The religions of the world are the ejaculations of a few imaginative men.

But the quality of the imagination is to flow, and not to freeze. The poet did not stop at the color, or the form, but read their meaning; neither may he rest in this meaning, but he makes the same objects exponents of his new thought. Here is the difference betwixt the poet and the mystic, that the last nails a symbol to one sense, which was a true sense for a moment, but soon becomes old and false. For all symbols are fluxional; all language is vehicular and transitive, and is good, as ferries and horses are, for conveyance, not as farms and houses are, for homestead. Mysticism consists in the mistake of an accidental and individual symbol for an universal one. The morning-redness happens to be the favorite meteor to the eyes of Jacob Behmen, and comes to stand to him for truth and faith; and he believes should stand for the same realities to every reader. But the first reader prefers as naturally the symbol of a mother and child, or a gardener and his bulb, or a jeweller polishing a gem. Either of these, or of a myriad more, are equally good to the person to whom they are significant. Only they must be held lightly, and be very willingly translated into the equivalent terms which others use. And the mystic must be steadily told,—All that you say is just as true without the tedious use of that symbol as with it. Let us have a little algebra, instead of this trite rhetoric,—universal signs, instead of these village symbols,—and we shall both be gainers. The history of hierarchies seems to show, that all religious error consisted in making the symbol too stark and solid, and, at last, nothing but an excess of the organ of language.

Swedenborg, of all men in the recent ages, stands eminently for the translator of nature into thought. I do not know the man in history to whom things stood so uniformly for words. Before him the metamorphosis continually plays. Everything on which his eye rests, obeys the impulses of moral nature. The figs become grapes whilst he eats them. When some of his angels affirmed a truth, the laurel twig which they held blossomed in their hands. The noise which, at a distance, appeared like gnashing and thumping, on coming nearer was found to be the voice of disputants. The men, in one of his visions, seen in heavenly light, appeared like dragons, and seemed in darkness: but, to each other, they appeared as men, and, when the light from heaven shone into their cabin, they complained of the darkness, and were compelled to shut the window that they might see.

There was this perception in him, which makes the poet or seer, an object of awe and terror, namely, that the same man, or society of men, may wear one aspect to themselves and their companions, and a different aspect to higher intelligences. Certain priests, whom he describes as conversing very learnedly together, appeared to the children, who were at some distance, like dead horses: and many the like misappearances. And instantly the mind inquires, whether these fishes under the bridge, yonder oxen in the pasture, those dogs in the yard, are immutably fishes, oxen, and dogs, or only so appear to me, and perchance to themselves appear upright men; and whether I appear as a man to all eyes. The Bramins and Pythagoras propounded the same question, and if any poet has witnessed the transformation, he doubtless found it in harmony with various experiences. We have all seen changes as considerable in wheat and caterpillars. He is the poet, and shall draw us with love and terror, who sees, through the flowing vest, the firm nature, and can declare it.

I look in vain for the poet whom I describe. We do not, with sufficient plainness, or sufficient profoundness, address ourselves to life, nor dare we chaunt our own times and social circumstance. If we filled the day with bravery, we should not shrink from celebrating it. Time and nature yield us many gifts, but not yet the timely man, the new religion, the reconciler, whom all things await. Dante's praise is, that he dared to write his autobiography in colossal cipher, or into universality. We have yet had no genius in America, with tyrannous eye, which knew the value of our incomparable materials, and saw, in the barbarism and materialism of the times, another carnival of the same gods whose picture he so much admires in Homer; then in the middle age; then in Calvinism. Banks and tariffs, the newspaper and caucus, methodism and unitarianism, are flat and dull to dull people, but rest on the same foundations of wonder as the town of Troy, and the temple of Delphos, and are as swiftly passing away. Our logrolling, our stumps and their politics, our fisheries, our Negroes, and Indians, our boats, and our repudiations, the wrath of rogues, and the pusillanimity of honest men, the northern trade, the southern planting, the western clearing, Oregon, and Texas, are yet unsung. Yet America is a poem in our eyes; its ample geography dazzles the imagination, and it will not wait long for metres. If I have not found that excellent combination of gifts in my countrymen which I seek, neither could I aid myself to fix the idea of the poet by reading now and then in Chalmers's collection of five centuries of English poets. These are wits, more than poets, though there have been poets among them. But when we adhere to the ideal of the poet, we have our difficulties even with Milton and Homer. Milton is too literary, and Homer too literal and historical.

But I am not wise enough for a national criticism, and must use the old largeness a little longer, to discharge my errand from the muse to the poet concerning his art.

Art is the path of the creator to his work. The paths, or methods, are ideal and eternal.

though few men ever see them, not the artist himself for years, or for a lifetime, unless he come into the conditions. The painter, the sculptor, the composer, the epic rhapsodist, the orator, all partake one desire, namely, to express themselves symmetrically and abundantly, not dwarfishly and fragmentarily. They found or put themselves in certain conditions, as, the painter and sculptor before some impressive human figures; the orator, into the assembly of the people; and the others, in such scenes as each has found exciting to his intellect; and each presently feels the new desire. He hears a voice, he sees a beckoning. Then he is apprised, with wonder, what herds of dæmons hem him in. He can no more rest; he says, with the old painter, " By God, it is in me, and must go forth of me." He pursues a beauty, half seen, which flies before him. The poet pours out verses in every solitude. Most of the things he says are conventional, no doubt; but by and by he says something which is original and beautiful. That charms him. He would say nothing else but such things. In our way of talking, we say, ' That is yours, this is mine;' but the poet knows well that it is not his; that it is as strange and beautiful to him as to you; he would fain hear the like eloquence at length. Once having tasted this immortal ichor, he cannot have enough of it, and, as an admirable creative power exists in these intellections, it is of the last importance that these things get spoken. What a little of all we know is said! What drops of all the sea of our science are baled up! and by what accident it is that these are exposed, when so many secrets sleep in nature! Hence the necessity of speech and song; hence these throbs and heart-beatings in the orator, at the door of the assembly, to the end, namely, that thought may be ejaculated as Logos, or Word.

Doubt not, O poet, but persist. Say, ' It is in me, and shall out.' Stand there, baulked and dumb, stuttering and stammering, hissed and hooted, stand and strive, until, at last, rage draw out of thee that *dream*-power which every night shows thee is thine own; a power transcending all limit and privacy, and by virtue of which a man is the conductor of the whole river of electricity. Nothing walks, or creeps, or grows, or exists, which must not in turn arise and walk before him as exponent of his mean-

ing. Comes he to that power, his genius is no
longer exhaustible. All the creatures, by pairs
and by tribes, pour into his mind as into a
Noah's ark, to come forth again to people a
new world. This is like the stock of air for our
respiration, or for the combustion of our fire-
place, not a measure of gallons, but the entire
atmosphere if wanted. And therefore the rich
poets, as Homer, Chaucer, Shakspeare, and Ra-
phael, have obviously no limits to their works,
except the limits of their lifetime, and resemble
a mirror carried through the street, ready to
render an image of every created thing.

O poet! a new nobility is conferred in groves
and pastures, and not in castles, or by the sword-
blade, any longer. The conditions are hard,
but equal. Thou shalt leave the world, and
know the muse only. Thou shalt not know
any longer the times, customs, graces, politics,
or opinions of men, but shalt take all from the
muse. For the time of towns is tolled from the
world by funereal chimes, but in nature the
universal hours are counted by succeeding tribes
of animals and plants, and by growth of joy on
joy. God wills also that thou abdicate a manifold and duplex life, and that thou be content

that others speak for thee. Others shall be thy
gentlemen, and shall represent all courtesy and
worldly life for thee; others shall do the great
and resounding actions also. Thou shalt lie
close hid with nature, and canst not be afforded
to the Capitol or the Exchange. The world is
full of renunciations and apprenticeships, and
this is thine: thou must pass for a fool and a
churl for a long season. This is the screen and
sheath in which Pan has protected his well-be-
loved flower, and thou shalt be known only to
thine own, and they shall console thee with
tenderest love. And thou shalt not be able to
rehearse the names of thy friends in thy verse,
for an old shame before the holy ideal. And
this is the reward: that the ideal shall be real
to thee, and the impressions of the actual world
shall fall like summer rain, copious, but not
troublesome, to thy invulnerable essence. Thou
shalt have the whole land for thy park and
manor, the sea for thy bath and navigation,
without tax and without envy; the woods and
the rivers thou shalt own; and thou shalt possess that wherein others are only tenants and
boarders. Thou true land-lord! sea-lord! air-
lord! Wherever snow falls, or water flows, or

birds fly, wherever day and night meet in twilight, wherever the blue heaven is hung by clouds, or sown with stars, wherever are forms with transparent boundaries, wherever are outlets into celestial space, wherever is danger, and awe, and love, there is Beauty, plenteous as rain, shed for thee, and though thou shouldest walk the world over, thou shalt not be able to find a condition inopportune or ignoble.

29

EXPERIENCE.

THE lords of life, the lords of life,—
I saw them pass,
In their own guise,
Like and unlike,
Portly and grim,
Use and Surprise,
Surface and Dream,
Succession swift, and spectral Wrong,
Temperament without a tongue,
And the inventor of the game
Omnipresent without name ;—
Some to see, some to be guessed,
They marched from east to west :
Little man, least of all,
Among the legs of his guardians tall,
Walked about with puzzled look :—
Him by the hand dear nature took ;
Dearest nature, strong and kind,
Whispered, ' Darling, never mind !
To-morrow they will wear another face,
The founder thou ! these are thy race ! '

ESSAY II.

EXPERIENCE.

———

WHERE do we find ourselves? In a series of which we do not know the extremes, and believe that it has none. We wake and find ourselves on a stair; there are stairs below us, which we seem to have ascended; there are stairs above us, many a one, which go upward and out of sight. But the Genius which, according to the old belief, stands at the door by which we enter, and gives us the lethe to drink, that we may tell no tales, mixed the cup too strongly, and we cannot shake off the lethargy now at noonday. Sleep lingers all our lifetime about our eyes, as night hovers all day in the boughs of the fir-tree. All things swim and glitter. Our life is not so much threatened as our perception. Ghost-like we glide through nature, and should not know our place again. Did our birth fall in some fit of indigence and frugality in nature, that she was so sparing of her fire and so liberal of her earth, that it appears to us that we lack the affirmative principle, and though we have health and reason, yet we have no superfluity of spirit for new creation? We have enough to live and bring the year about, but not an ounce to impart or to invest. Ah that our Genius were a little more of a genius! We are like millers on the lower levels of a stream, when the factories above them have exhausted the water. We too fancy that the upper people must have raised their dams.

If any of us knew what we were doing, or where we are going, then when we think we best know! We do not know to-day whether we are busy or idle. In times when we thought ourselves indolent, we have afterwards discovered, that much was accomplished, and much was begun in us. All our days are so unprofitable while they pass, that 'tis wonderful where or when we ever got anything of this which we call wisdom, poetry, virtue. We never got it on any dated calendar day. Some heavenly days must have been intercalated somewhere, like those that Hermes won with dice of the Moon, that Osiris might be born. It is said, all martyrdoms looked mean when they were suffered. Every ship is a romantic object, except that we sail in. Embark, and the romance quits our vessel, and hangs on every other sail in the horizon. Our life looks trivial, and we shun to record it. Men seem to have learned of the horizon the art of perpetual retreating and reference. 'Yonder uplands are rich pasturage, and my neighbor has fertile meadow, but my field,' says the querulous farmer, 'only holds the world together.' I quote another man's saying; unluckily, that other withdraws himself in the same way, and quotes me. ' 'Tis the trick of nature thus to degrade to-day; a good deal of buzz, and somewhere a result slipped magically in. Every roof is agreeable to the eye, until it is lifted; then we find tragedy and moaning women, and hard-eyed husbands, and deluges of lethe, and the men ask, 'What's the news?' as if the old were so bad. How many individuals can we count in society? how many actions? how many opinions? So much of our time is preparation, so much is routine, and so much retrospect, that the pith of each man's genius contracts itself to a very few hours. The history of literature—take the net result of

Tiraboschi, Warton, or Schlegel,—is a sum of very few ideas, and of very few original tales,— all the rest being variation of these. So in this great society wide lying around us, a critical analysis would find very few spontaneous actions. It is almost all custom and gross sense. There are even few opinions, and these seem organic in the speakers, and do not disturb the universal necessity.

What opium is instilled into all disaster! It shows formidable as we approach it, but there is at last no rough rasping friction, but the most slippery sliding surfaces. We fall soft on a thought. *Ate Dea* is gentle,

> "Over men's heads walking aloft,
> With tender feet treading so soft."

People grieve and bemoan themselves, but it is not half so bad with them as they say. There are moods in which we court suffering, in the hope that here, at least, we shall find reality, sharp peaks and edges of truth. But it turns out to be scene-painting and counterfeit. The only thing grief has taught me, is to know how shallow it is. That, like all the rest, plays about the surface, and never introduces me into

the reality, for contact with which, we would
even pay the costly price of sons and lovers.
Was it Boscovich who found out that bodies
never come in contact? Well, souls never
touch their objects. An innavigable sea washes
with silent waves between us and the things we
aim at and converse with. Grief too will make
us idealists. In the death of my son, now more
than two years ago, I seem to have lost a beautiful estate,—no more. I cannot get it nearer
to me. If to-morrow I should be informed of
the bankruptcy of my principal debtors, the
loss of my property would be a great inconvenience to me, perhaps, for many years; but it
would leave me as it found me,—neither better
nor worse. So is it with this calamity: it does
not touch me: some thing which I fancied was
a part of me, which could not be torn away
without tearing me, nor enlarged without en-
riching me, falls off from me, and leaves no
scar. It was caducous. I grieve that grief
can teach me nothing, nor carry me one step
into real nature. The Indian who was laid
under a curse, that the wind should not blow
on him, nor water flow to him, nor fire burn
him, is a type of us all. The dearest events are

summer-rain, and we the Para coats that shed every drop. Nothing is left us now but death. We look to that with a grim satisfaction, saying, there at least is reality that will not dodge us.

I take this evanescence and lubricity of all objects, which lets them slip through our fingers then when we clutch hardest, to be the most unhandsome part of our condition. Nature does not like to be observed, and likes that we should be her fools and playmates. We may have the sphere for our cricket-ball, but not a berry for our philosophy. Direct strokes she never gave us power to make; all our blows glance, all our hits are accidents. Our relations to each other are oblique and casual.

Dream delivers us to dream, and there is no end to illusion. Life is a train of moods like a string of beads, and as we pass through them, they prove to be many-colored lenses which paint the world their own hue, and each shows only what lies in its focus. From the mountain you see the mountain. We animate what we can, and we see only what we animate. Nature and books belong to the eyes that see them

It depends on the mood of the man, whether he shall see the sunset or the fine poem. There are always sunsets, and there is always genius; but only a few hours so serene that we can relish nature or criticism. The more or less depends on structure or temperament. Temperament is the iron wire on which the beads are strung. Of what use is fortune or talent to a cold and defective nature? Who cares what sensibility or discrimination a man has at some time shown, if he falls asleep in his chair? or if he laugh and giggle? or if he apologize? or is affected with egotism? or thinks of his dollar? or cannot go by food? or has gotten a child in his boyhood? Of what use is genius, if the organ is too convex or too concave, and cannot find a focal distance within the actual horizon of human life? Of what use, if the brain is too cold or too hot, and the man does not care enough for results, to stimulate him to experiment, and hold him up in it? or if the web is too finely woven, too irritable by pleasure and pain, so that life stagnates from too much reception, without due outlet? Of what use to make heroic vows of amendment, if the same old lawbreaker is to keep them? What cheer can the religious sentiment yield, when that is suspected to be secretly dependent on the seasons of the year, and the state of the blood? I knew a witty physician who found theology in the biliary duct, and used to affirm that if there was disease in the liver, the man became a Calvinist, and if that organ was sound, he became a Unitarian. Very mortifying is the reluctant experience that some unfriendly excess or imbecility neutralizes the promise of genius. We see young men who owe us a new world, so readily and lavishly they promise, but they never acquit the debt; they die young and dodge the account: or if they live, they lose themselves in the crowd.

Temperament also enters fully into the system of illusions, and shuts us in a prison of glass which we cannot see. There is an optical illusion about every person we meet. In truth, they are all creatures of given temperament, which will appear in a given character, whose boundaries they will never pass: but we look at them, they seem alive, and we presume there is impulse in them. In the moment it seems impulse; in the year, in the lifetime, it turns out to be a certain uniform tune which the revolving barrel of the music-box must play. Men resist the conclusion in the morning, but adopt it as the evening wears on, that temper prevails over everything of time, place, and condition, and is inconsumable in the flames of religion. Some modifications the moral sentiment avails to impose, but the individual texture holds its dominion, if not to bias the moral judgments, yet to fix the measure of activity and of enjoyment.

I thus express the law as it is read from the platform of ordinary life, but must not leave it without noticing the capital exception. For temperament is a power which no man willingly hears any one praise but himself. On the platform of physics, we cannot resist the contracting influences of so-called science. Temperament puts all divinity to rout. I know the mental proclivity of physicians. I hear the chuckle of the phrenologists. Theoretic kidnappers and slave-drivers, they esteem each man the victim of another, who winds him round his finger by knowing the law of his being, and by such cheap signboards as the color of his beard, or the slope of his occiput, reads the inventory of his fortunes and character. The grossest ignorance does not disgust like this impudent knowingness. The physicians say, they are not materialists; but they are:—Spirit is matter reduced to an extreme thinness: O *so* thin!—But the definition of *spiritual* should be, *that which is its own evidence*. What notions do they attach to love! what to religion! One would not willingly pronounce these words in their hearing, and give them the occasion to profane them. I saw a gracious gentleman who adapts his conversation to the form of the head of the man he talks with! I had fancied that the value of life lay in its inscrutable possibilities; in the fact that I never know, in addressing myself to a new individual, what may befall me. I carry the keys of my castle in my hand, ready to throw them at the feet of my lord, whenever and in what disguise soever he shall appear. I know he is in the neighborhood hidden among vagabonds. Shall I preclude my future, by taking a high seat, and kindly adapting my conversation to the shape of heads? When I come to that, the doctors shall buy me for a cent. —— 'But, sir, medical history; the report to the Institute; the proven facts!'—I distrust the facts and the inferences. Temperament is the veto or limitation-power in the constitution, very justly applied to restrain an opposite excess in the constitution, but absurdly offered as a bar to original equity. When virtue is in presence, all subordinate powers sleep. On its own level, or in view of nature, temperament is final. I see not, if one be once caught in this trap of so-called sciences, any escape for the man from the links of the chain of physical necessity. Given such an embryo, such a history must follow. On this platform, one lives in a sty of sensualism, and would soon come to suicide. But it is impossible that the creative power should exclude itself. Into every intelligence there is a door which is never closed, through which the creator passes. The intellect, seeker of absolute truth, or the heart, lover of absolute good, intervenes for our succor, and at one whisper of these high powers, we awake from ineffectual struggles with this nightmare. We hurl it into its own hell, and cannot again contract ourselves to so base a state.

The secret of the illusoriness is in the ne-

cessity of a succession of moods or objects.
Gladly we would anchor, but the anchorage is
quicksand. This onward trick of nature is too
strong for us: *Pero si muove*. When, at night,
I look at the moon and stars, I seem stationary,
and they to hurry. Our love of the real draws
us to permanence, but health of body consists
in circulation, and sanity of mind in variety or
facility of association. We need change of
objects. Dedication to one thought is quickly
odious. We house with the insane, and must
humor them; then conversation dies out.
Once I took such delight in Montaigne, that I
thought I should not need any other book; before that, in Shakspeare; then in Plutarch; then
in Plotinus; at one time in Bacon; afterwards
in Goethe; even in Bettine; but now I turn the
pages of either of them languidly, whilst I still
cherish their genius. So with pictures; each
will bear an emphasis of attention once, which
it cannot retain, though we fain would continue
to be pleased in that manner. How strongly I
have felt of pictures, that when you have seen
one well, you must take your leave of it; you
shall never see it again. I have had good lessons from pictures, which I have since seen

without emotion or remark. A deduction must be made from the opinion, which even the wise express of a new book or occurrence. Their opinion gives me tidings of their mood, and some vague guess at the new fact, but is nowise to be trusted as the lasting relation between that intellect and that thing. The child asks, ' Mamma, why don't I like the story as well as when you told it me yesterday?' Alas, child, it is even so with the oldest cherubim of knowledge. But will it answer thy question to say, Because thou wert born to a whole, and this story is a particular? The reason of the pain this discovery causes us (and we make it late in respect to works of art and intellect), is the plaint of tragedy which murmurs from it in regard to persons, to friendship and love.

That immobility and absence of elasticity which we find in the arts, we find with more pain in the artist. There is no power of expansion in men. Our friends early appear to us as representatives of certain ideas, which they never pass or exceed. They stand on the brink of the ocean of thought and power, but they never take the single step that would bring them there. A man is like a bit of Labrador

30

spar, which has no lustre as you turn it in your hand, until you come to a particular angle; then it shows deep and beautiful colors. There is no adaptation or universal applicability in men, but each has his special talent, and the mastery of successful men consists in adroitly keeping themselves where and when that turn shall be oftenest to be practised. We do what we must, and call it by the best names we can, and would fain have the praise of having intended the result which ensues. I cannot recall any form of man who is not superfluous sometimes. But is not this pitiful? Life is not worth the taking, to do tricks in.

Of course, it needs the whole society, to give the symmetry we seek. The parti-colored wheel must revolve very fast to appear white. Something is learned too by conversing with so much folly and defect. In fine, whoever loses, we are always of the gaining party. Divinity is behind our failures and follies also. The plays of children are nonsense, but very educative nonsense. So it is with the largest and solemnest things, with commerce, government, church, marriage, and so with the history of every man's bread, and the ways by which he

is to come by it.   Like a bird which alights
nowhere, but hops perpetually from bough to
bough, is the Power which abides in no man
and in no woman, but for a moment speaks
from this one, and for another moment from
that one.

But what help from these fineries or pedan-
tries?   What help from thought?   Life is not
dialectics.   We, I think, in these times, have
had lessons enough of the futility of criticism.
Our young people have thought and written
much on labor and reform, and for all that they
have written, neither the world nor themselves
have got on a step.   Intellectual tasting of life
will not supersede muscular activity.   If a man
should consider the nicety of the passage of a
piece of bread down his throat, he would starve.
At Education-Farm, the noblest theory of life
sat on the noblest figures of young men and
maidens, quite powerless and melancholy.   It
would not rake or pitch a ton of hay; it would
not rub down a horse; and the men and
maidens it left pale and hungry.   A political
orator wittily compared our party promises to
western roads, which opened stately enough,

with planted trees on either side, to tempt the traveller, but soon became narrow and narrower, and ended in a squirrel-track, and ran up a tree. So does culture with us; it ends in head-ache. Unspeakably sad and barren does life look to those, who a few months ago were dazzled with the splendor of the promise of the times. " There is now no longer any right course of action, nor any self-devotion left among the Iranis." Objections and criticism we have had our fill of. There are objections to every course of life and action, and the practical wisdom infers an indifferency, from the omnipresence of objection. The whole frame of things preaches indifferency. Do not craze yourself with thinking, but go about your business anywhere. Life is not intellectual or critical, but sturdy. Its chief good is for well-mixed people who can enjoy what they find, without question. Nature hates peeping, and our mothers speak her very sense when they say, " Children, eat your victuals, and say no more of it." To fill the hour,—that is happiness ; to fill the hour, and leave no crevice for a repentance or an approval. We live amid surfaces, and the true art of life is to skate well on them. Under the oldest mouldiest conventions, a man of native force prospers just as well as in the newest world, and that by skill of handling and treatment. He can take hold anywhere. Life itself is a mixture of power and form, and will not bear the least excess of either. To finish the moment, to find the journey's end in every step of the road, to live the greatest number of good hours, is wisdom. It is not the part of men, but of fanatics, or of mathematicians, if you will, to say, that, the shortness of life considered, it is not worth caring whether for so short a duration we were sprawling in want, or sitting high. Since our office is with moments, let us husband them. Five minutes of to-day are worth as much to me, as five minutes in the next millennium. Let us be poised, and wise, and our own, to-day. Let us treat the men and women well: treat them as if they were real: perhaps they are. Men live in their fancy, like drunkards whose hands are too soft and tremulous for successful labor. It is a tempest of fancies, and the only ballast I know, is a respect to the present hour. Without any shadow of doubt, amidst this vertigo of shows and politics, I settle myself ever the firmer in the creed, that we should not

postpone and refer and wish, but do broad
justice where we are, by whomsoever we deal
with, accepting our actual companions and circumstances, however humble or odious, as the
mystic officials to whom the universe has del-
egated its whole pleasure for us.   If these are
mean and malignant, their contentment, which
is the last victory of justice, is a more satisfying
echo to the heart, than the voice of poets and
the casual sympathy of admirable persons.   I
think that however a thoughtful man may
suffer from the defects and absurdities of his
company, he cannot without affectation deny to
any set of men and women, a sensibility to extraordinary merit.   The coarse and frivolous
have an instinct of superiority, if they have not
a sympathy, and honor it in their blind capri-
cious way with sincere homage.

The fine young people despise life, but in me,
and in such as with me are free from dyspepsia,
and to whom a day is a sound and solid good,
it is a great excess of politeness to look scorn-
ful and to cry for company.   I am grown by
sympathy a little eager and sentimental, but
leave me alone, and I should relish every
hour and what it brought me, the potluck of

the day, as heartily as the oldest gossip in the bar-room. I am thankful for small mercies. I compared notes with one of my friends who expects everything of the universe, and is disappointed when anything is less than the best, and I found that I begin at the other extreme, expecting nothing, and am always full of thanks for moderate goods. I accept the clangor and jangle of contrary tendencies. I find my account in sots and bores also. They give a reality to the circumjacent picture, which such a vanishing meteorous appearance can ill spare. In the morning I awake, and find the old world, wife, babes, and mother, Concord and Boston, the dear old spiritual world, and even the dear old devil not far off. If we will take the good we find, asking no questions, we shall have heaping measures. The great gifts are not got by analysis. Everything good is on the highway. The middle region of our being is the temperate zone. We may climb into the thin and cold realm of pure geometry and lifeless science, or sink into that of sensation. Between these extremes is the equator of life, of thought, of spirit, of poetry,—a narrow belt. Moreover, in popular experience, everything good is on

the highway. A collector peeps into all the
picture-shops of Europe, for a landscape of
Poussin, a crayon-sketch of Salvator; but
the Transfiguration, the Last Judgment, the
Communion of St. Jerome, and what are as
transcendent as these, are on the walls of the
Vatican, the Uffizii, or the Louvre, where every
footman may see them; to say nothing of
nature's pictures in every street, of sunsets and
sunrises every day, and the sculpture of the
human body never absent. A collector recently
bought at public auction, in London, for one
hundred and fifty-seven guineas, an autograph
of Shakspeare: but for nothing a school-boy
can read Hamlet, and can detect secrets of
highest concernment yet unpublished therein.
I think I will never read any but the commonest
books,—the Bible, Homer, Dante, Shakspeare,
and Milton. Then we are impatient of so public
a life and planet, and run hither and thither for
nooks and secrets. The imagination delights in
the woodcraft of Indians, trappers, and bee-
hunters. We fancy that we are strangers, and
not so intimately domesticated in the planet as
the wild man, and the wild beast and bird. But
the exclusion reaches them also; reaches the

climbing, flying, gliding, feathered and four-footed man. Fox and woodchuck, hawk and snipe, and bittern, when nearly seen, have no more root in the deep world than man, and are just such superficial tenants of the globe. Then the new molecular philosophy shows astronomical interspaces betwixt atom and atom, shows that the world is all outside: it has no inside.

The mid-world is best. Nature, as we know her, is no saint. The lights of the church, the ascetics, Gentoos and Grahamites, she does not distinguish by any favor. She comes eating and drinking and sinning. Her darlings, the great, the strong, the beautiful, are not children of our law, do not come out of the Sunday School, nor weigh their food, nor punctually keep the commandments. If we will be strong with her strength, we must not harbor such disconsolate consciences, borrowed too from the consciences of other nations. We must set up the strong present tense against all the rumors of wrath, past or to come. So many things are unsettled which it is of the first importance to settle,—and, pending their settlement, we will do as we do. Whilst the debate goes forward on the equity of commerce, and will not be closed for a century or two, New and Old England may keep shop. Law of copyright and international copyright is to be discussed, and, in the interim, we will sell our books for the most we can. Expediency of literature, reason of literature, lawfulness of writing down a thought, is questioned; much is to say on both sides, and, while the fight waxes hot, thou, dearest scholar, stick to thy foolish task, add a line every hour, and between whiles add a line. Right to hold land, right of property, is disputed, and the conventions convene, and before the vote is taken, dig away in your garden, and spend your earnings as a waif or godsend to all serene and beautiful purposes. Life itself is a bubble and a skepticism, and a sleep within a sleep. Grant it, and as much more as they will,—but thou, God's darling! heed thy private dream: thou wilt not be missed in the scorning and skepticism: there are enough of them: stay there in thy closet, and toil, until the rest are agreed what to do about it. Thy sickness, they say, and thy puny habit, require that thou do this or avoid that, but know that thy life is a flitting state, a tent for a night, and do thou, sick or well, finish that stint. Thou art sick, but shalt not be worse, and the universe, which holds thee dear, shall be the better.

Human life is made up of the two elements, power and form, and the proportion must be invariably kept, if we would have it sweet and sound. Each of these elements in excess makes a mischief as hurtful as its defect. Everything runs to excess: every good quality is noxious, if unmixed, and, to carry the danger to the edge of ruin, nature causes each man's peculiarity to superabound. Here, among the farms, we adduce the scholars as examples of this treachery. They are nature's victims of expression. You who see the artist, the orator, the poet, too near, and find their life no more excellent than that of mechanics or farmers, and themselves victims of partiality, very hollow and haggard, and pronounce them failures,— not heroes, but quacks,—conclude very reasonably, that these arts are not for man, but are disease. Yet nature will not bear you out. Irresistible nature made men such, and makes legions more of such, every day. You love the boy reading in a book, gazing at a drawing, or a cast: yet what are these millions who read and behold, but incipient writers and sculptors?

Add a little more of that quality which now reads and sees, and they will seize the pen and chisel.   And if one remembers how innocently he began to be an artist, he perceives that nature joined with his enemy.   A man is a golden impossibility.   The line he must walk is a hair's breadth.   The wise through excess of wisdom is made a fool.

How easily, if fate would suffer it, we might keep forever these beautiful limits, and adjust ourselves, once for all, to the perfect calculation of the kingdom of known cause and effect.   In the street and in the newspapers, life appears so plain a business, that manly resolution and adherence to the multiplication-table through all weathers, will insure success.   But ah! presently comes a day, or is it only a half-hour, with its angel-whispering,—which discomfits the conclusions of nations and of years!   Tomorrow again, everything looks real and angular, the habitual standards are reinstated, common sense is as rare as genius,—is the basis of genius, and experience is hands and feet to every enterprise;—and yet, he who should do his business on this understanding, would be quickly bankrupt. Power keeps quite another road than the turnpikes of choice and will, namely, the subterranean and invisible tunnels and channels of life. It is ridiculous that we are diplomatists, and doctors, and considerate people: there are no dupes like these. Life is a series of surprises, and would not be worth taking or keeping, if it were not. God delights to isolate us every day, and hide from us the past and the future. We would look about us, but with grand politeness he draws down before us an impenetrable screen of purest sky, and another behind us of purest sky. 'You will not remember,' he seems to say, 'and you will not expect.' All good conversation, manners, and action, come from a spontaneity which forgets usages, and makes the moment great. Nature hates calculators; her methods are saltatory and impulsive. Man lives by pulses; our organic movements are such; and the chemical and ethereal agents are undulatory and alternate; and the mind goes antagonizing on, and never prospers but by fits. We thrive by casualties. Our chief experiences have been casual. The most attractive class of people are those who are powerful obliquely, and not by the

direct stroke: men of genius, but not yet ac-
credited: one gets the cheer of their light, without paying too great a tax. Theirs is the
beauty of the bird, or the morning light, and
not of art. In the thought of genius there is
always a surprise; and the moral sentiment is
well called " the newness," for it is never other;
as new to the oldest intelligence as to the young
child,—" the kingdom that cometh without
observation." In like manner, for practical success, there must not be too much design. A
man will not be observed in doing that which he
can do best. There is a certain magic about his
properest action, which stupefies your powers
of observation, so that though it is done before
you, you wist not of it. The art of life has
a pudency, and will not be exposed. Every
man is an impossibility, until he is born; every
thing impossible, until we see a success. The
ardors of piety agree at last with the coldest
skepticism,—that nothing is of us or our
works,—that all is of God. Nature will not
spare us the smallest leaf of laurel. All writing comes by the grace of God, and all doing
and having. I would gladly be moral, and keep
due metes and bounds, which I dearly love,

and allow the most to the will of man, but I
have set my heart on honesty in this chapter,
and I can see nothing at last, in success or
failure, than more or less of vital force sup-
plied from the Eternal. The results of life
are uncalculated and uncalculable. The years
teach much which the days never know.
The persons who compose our company, converse, and come and go, and design and execute
many things, and somewhat comes of it all, but
an unlooked for result. The individual is
always mistaken. He designed many things,
and drew in other persons as coadjutors, quar-
relled with some or all, blundered much, and
something is done; all are a little advanced, but
the individual is always mistaken. It turns out
somewhat new, and very unlike what he promised himself.

The ancients, struck with this irreducibleness
of the elements of human life to calculation, ex-
alted Chance into a divinity, but that is to stay
too long at the spark,—which glitters truly at
one point,—but the universe is warm with the
latency of the same fire. The miracle of life
which will not be expounded, but will remain a

miracle, introduces a new element. In the growth of the embryo, Sir Everard Home, I think, noticed that the evolution was not from one central point, but co-active from three or more points. Life has no memory. That which proceeds in succession might be remembered, but that which is co-existent, or ejaculated from a deeper cause, as yet far from being conscious, knows not its own tendency. So is it with us, now skeptical, or without unity, because immersed in forms and effects all seeming to be of equal yet hostile value, and now religious, whilst in the reception of spiritual law. Bear with these distractions, with this coetaneous growth of the parts: they will one day be *members*, and obey one will. On that one will, on that secret cause, they nail our attention and hope. Life is hereby melted into an expectation or a religion. Underneath the inharmonious and trivial particulars, is a musical perfection, the Ideal journeying always with us, the heaven without rent or seam. Do but observe the mode of our illumination. When I converse with a profound mind, or if at any time being alone I have good thoughts, I do not at once arrive at satisfactions, as when, being thirsty, I drink water, or go to the fire, being cold: no! but I am at first apprised of my vicinity to a new and excellent region of life. By persisting to read or to think, this region gives further sign of itself, as it were in flashes of light, in sudden discoveries of its profound beauty and repose, as if the clouds that covered it parted at intervals, and showed the approaching traveller the inland mountains, with the tranquil eternal meadows spread at their base, whereon flocks graze, and shepherds pipe and dance. But every insight from this realm of thought is felt as initial, and promises a sequel. I do not make it; I arrive there, and behold what was there already. I make! O no! I clap my hands in infantine joy and amazement, before the first opening to me of this august magnificence, old with the love and homage of innumerable ages, young with the life of life, the sunbright Mecca of the desert. And what a future it opens! I feel a new heart beating with the love of the new beauty. I am ready to die out of nature, and be born again into this new yet unapproachable America I have found in the West.

31

"Since neither now nor yesterday began
  These thoughts, which have been ever, nor yet can
  A man be found who their first entrance knew."

If I have described life as a flux of moods, I
mnst now add, that there is that in us which
changes not, and which ranks all sensations
and states of mind.   The consciousness in each
man is a sliding scale, which identifies him now
with the First Cause, and now with the flesh of
his body; life above life, in infinite degrees.
The sentiment from which it sprung determines
the dignity of any deed, and the question ever
is, not, what you have done or forborne, but, at
whose command you have done or forborne it.

Fortune, Minerva, Muse, Holy Ghost,—
these are quaint names, too narrow to cover
this unbounded substance.   The baffled intellect must still kneel before this cause, which
refuses to be named,—ineffable cause, which
every fine genius has essayed to represent by
some emphatic symbol, as, Thales by water,
Anaximenes by air, Anaxagoras by (Νους)
thought, Zoroaster by fire, Jesus and the mod-
erns by love: and the metaphor of each has
become a national religion.   The Chinese Mencius has not been the least successful in his

generalization. "I fully understand language,"
he said, "and nourish well my vast-flowing
vigor."—"I beg to ask what you call vast-flowing vigor?"—said his companion. "The explanation," replied Mencius, "is difficult. This vigor
is supremely great, and in the highest degree
unbending. Nourish it correctly, and do it no
injury, and it will fill up the vacancy between
heaven and earth. This vigor accords with and
assists justice and reason, and leaves no hunger."
—In our more correct writing, we give to this
generalization the name of Being, and thereby
confess that we have arrived as far as we can
go. Suffice it for the joy of the universe, that
we have not arrived at a wall, but at interminable
oceans. Our life seems not present, so much
as prospective; not for the affairs on which it is
wasted, but as a hint of this vast-flowing vigor.
Most of life seems to be mere advertisement of
faculty: information is given us not to sell ourselves cheap; that we are very great. So, in
particulars, our greatness is always in a tendency or direction, not in an action. It is for us
to believe in the rule, not in the exception.
The noble are thus known from the ignoble.
So in accepting the leading of the sentiments,

it is not what we believe concerning the immortality of the soul, or the like, but *the universal impulse to believe*, that is the material circumstance, and is the principal fact in the history of the globe. Shall we describe this cause as that which works directly? The spirit is not helpless or needful of mediate organs. It has plentiful powers and direct effects. I am explained without explaining, I am felt without acting, and where I am not. Therefore all just persons are satisfied with their own praise. They refuse to explain themselves, and are content that new actions should do them that office. They believe that we communicate without speech, and above speech, and that no right action of ours is quite unaffecting to our friends, at whatever distance; for the influence of action is not to be measured by miles. Why should I fret myself, because a circumstance has occurred, which hinders my presence where I was expected? If I am not at the meeting, my presence where I am, should be as useful to the commonwealth of friendship and wisdom, as would be my presence in that place. I exert the same quality of power in all places. Thus journeys the mighty

Ideal before us; it never was known to fall into the rear. No man ever came to an experience which was satiating, but his good is tidings of a better. Onward and onward! In liberated moments, we know that a new picture of life and duty is already possible ; the elements already exist in many minds around you, of a doctrine of life which shall transcend any written record we have. The new statement will comprise the skepticisms, as well as the faiths of a society, and out of unbeliefs a creed shall be formed. For, skepticisms are not gratuitous or lawless, but are limitations of the affirmative statement, and the new philosophy must take them in, and make affirmations outside of them, just as much as it must include the oldest beliefs.

It is very unhappy, but too late to be helped, the discovery we have made, that we exist. That discovery is called the Fall of Man. Ever afterwards, we suspect our instruments. We have learned that we do not see directly, but mediately, and that we have no means of correcting these colored and distorting lenses which we are, or of computing the amount of their errors. Perhaps these subject-lenses have a creative power; perhaps there are no objects. Once we lived in what we saw; now, the rapaciousness of this new power, which threatens to absorb all things, engages us. Nature, art, persons, letters, religions,—objects, successively tumble in, and God is but one of its ideas. Nature and literature are subjective phenomena; every evil and every good thing is a shadow which we cast. The street is full of humiliations to the proud. As the fop contrived to dress his bailiffs in his livery, and make them wait on his guests at table, so the chagrins which the bad heart gives off as bubbles, at once take form as ladies and gentlemen in the street, shopmen or barkeepers in hotels, and threaten or insult whatever is threatenable and insultable in us. 'Tis the same with our idolatries. People forget that it is the eye which makes the horizon, and the rounding mind's eye which makes this or that man a type or representative of humanity with the name of hero or saint. Jesus the "providential man," is a good man on whom many people are agreed that these optical laws shall take effect. By love on one part, and by forbearance to press objection on the other part, it is for a time settled, that we

will look at him in the centre of the horizon,
and ascribe to him the properties that will attach
to any man so seen. But the longest love or
aversion has a speedy term. The great and
crescive self, rooted in absolute nature, supplants
all relative existence, and ruins the kingdom of
mortal friendship and love. Marriage (in what
is called the spiritual world) is impossible, because of the inequality between every subject
and every object. The subject is the receiver
of Godhead, and at every comparison must feel
his being enhanced by that cryptic might.
Though not in energy, yet by presence, this
magazine of substance cannot be otherwise than
felt: nor can any force of intellect attribute to
the object the proper deity which sleeps or
wakes forever in every subject. Never can love
make consciousness and ascription equal in
force. There will be the same gulf between
every me and thee, as between the original and
the picture. The universe is the bride of the
soul. All private sympathy is partial. Two
human beings are like globes, which can touch
only in a point, and, whilst they remain in contact, all other points of each of the spheres are
inert; their turn must also come, and the longer

a particular union lasts, the more energy of appetency the parts not in union acquire.

Life will be imaged, but cannot be divided nor doubled. Any invasion of its unity would be chaos. The soul is not twin-born, but the only begotten, and though revealing itself as child in time, child in appearance, is of a fatal and universal power, admitting no co-life. Every day, every act betrays the ill-concealed deity. We believe in ourselves, as we do not believe in others. We permit all things to ourselves, and that which we call sin in others, is experiment for us. It is an instance of our faith in ourselves, that men never speak of crime as lightly as they think: or, every man thinks a latitude safe for himself, which is nowise to be indulged to another. The act looks very differently on the inside, and on the outside; in its quality, and in its consequences. Murder in the murderer is no such ruinous thought as poets and romancers will have it; it does not unsettle him, or fright him from his ordinary notice of trifles: it is an act quite easy to be contemplated, but in its sequel, it turns out to be a horrible jangle and confounding of all relations. Especially the crimes that spring from love, seem right and fair from the actor's point of view, but, when acted, are found destructive of society. No man at last believes that he can be lost, nor that the crime in him is as black as in the felon. Because the intellect qualifies in our own case the moral judgments. For there is no crime to the intellect. That is antinomian or hypernomian, and judges law as well as fact. "It is worse than a crime, it is a blunder," said Napoleon, speaking the language of the intellect. To it, the world is a problem in mathematics or the science of quantity, and it leaves out praise and blame, and all weak emotions. All stealing is comparative. If you come to absolutes, pray who does not steal? Saints are sad, because they behold sin, (even when they speculate,) from the point of view of the conscience, and not of the intellect; a confusion of thought. Sin seen from the thought, is a diminution or *less:* seen from the conscience or will, it is pravity or *bad*. The intellect names it shade, absence of light, and no essence. The conscience must feel it as essence, essential evil. This it is not: it has an objective existence, but no subjective.

Thus inevitably does the universe wear our

color, and every object fall successively into the subject itself. The subject exists, the subject enlarges; all things sooner or later fall into place. As I am, so I see; use what language we will, we can never say anything but what we are; Hermes, Cadmus, Columbus, Newton, Buonaparte, are the mind's ministers. Instead of .feeling a poverty when we encounter a great man, let us treat the new comer like a travelling geologist, who passes through our estate, and shows us good slate, or limestone, or anthracite, in our brush pasture. The partial action of each strong mind in one direction, is a telescope for the objects on which it is pointed. But every other part of knowledge is to be pushed to the same extravagance, ere the soul attains her due sphericity. Do you see that kitten chasing so prettily her own tail? If you could look with her eyes, you might see her surrounded with hundreds of figures performing complex dramas, with tragic and comic issues, long conversations, many characters, many ups and downs of fate,—and meantime it is only puss and her tail. How long before our masquerade will end its noise of tamborines, laughter, and shouting, and we shall find it was a solitary performance?—A subject and an object,—it takes so much to make the galvanic circuit complete, but magnitude adds nothing. What imports it whether it is Kepler and the sphere; Columbus and America; a reader and his book; or puss with her tail?

It is true that all the muses and love and religion hate these developments, and will find a way to punish the chemist, who publishes in the parlor the secrets of the laboratory. And we cannot say too little of our constitutional necessity of seeing things under private aspects, or saturated with our humors. And yet is the God the native of these bleak rocks. That need makes in morals the capital virtue of self-trust. We must hold hard to this poverty, however scandalous, and by more vigorous self-recoveries, after the sallies of action, possess our axis more firmly. The life of truth is cold, and so far mournful; but it is not the slave of tears, contritions, and perturbations. It does not attempt another's work, nor adopt another's facts. It is a main lesson of wisdom to know your own from another's. I have learned that I cannot dispose of other people's facts; but I possess such a key to my own, as persuades me against all their denials, that they also have a key to theirs. A sympathetic person is placed in the dilemma of a swimmer among drowning men, who all catch at him, and if he give so much as a leg or a finger, they will drown him. They wish to be saved from the mischiefs of their vices, but not from their vices. Charity would be wasted on this poor waiting on the symptoms. A wise and hardy physician will say, *Come out of that*, as the first condition of advice.

In this our talking America, we are ruined by our good nature and listening on all sides. This compliance takes away the power of being greatly useful. A man should not be able to look other than directly and forthright. A preoccupied attention is the only answer to the importunate frivolity of other people : an attention, and to an aim which makes their wants frivolous. This is a divine answer, and leaves no appeal, and no hard thoughts. In Flaxman's drawing of the Eumenides of Æschylus, Orestes supplicates Apollo, whilst the Furies sleep on the threshold. The face of the god expresses a shade of regret and compassion, but calm with the conviction of the irreconcilableness of the two spheres. He is born into other politics, into the eternal and beautiful. The man at his feet asks for his interest in turmoils of the earth, into which his nature cannot enter. And the Eumenides there lying express pictorially this disparity. The god is surcharged with his divine destiny.

Illusion, Temperament, Succession, Surface, Surprise, Reality, Subjectiveness,—these are threads on the loom of time, these are the lords of life. I dare not assume to give their order, but I name them as I find them in my way. I know better than to claim any completeness for my picture. I am a fragment, and this is a fragment of me. I can very confidently announce one or another law, which throws itself into relief and form, but I am too young yet by some ages to compile a code. I gossip for my hour concerning the eternal politics. I have seen many fair pictures not in vain. A wonderful time I have lived in. I am not the novice I was fourteen, nor yet seven years ago. Let who will ask, where is the fruit? I find a private fruit sufficient. This is a fruit,—that I should not ask for a rash effect from meditations, counsels, and the hiving of truths. I should feel it pitiful to demand a result on this town and county, an overt effect on the instant month and year. The effect is deep and secular as the cause. It works on periods in which mortal lifetime is lost. All I know is reception; I am and I have: but I do not get, and when I have fancied I had gotten anything, I found I did not. I worship with wonder the great Fortune. My reception has been so large, that I am not annoyed by receiving this or that superabundantly. I say to the Genius, if he will pardon the proverb, *In for a mill, in for a million.* When I receive a new gift, I do not macerate my body to make the account square, for, if I should die, I could not make the account square. The benefit overran the merit the first day, and has overran the merit ever since. The merit itself, so-called, I reckon part of the receiving.

Also, that hankering after an overt or practical effect seems to me an apostasy. In good earnest, I am willing to spare this most unnecessary deal of doing. Life wears to me a visionary face. Hardest, roughest action is visionary also. It is but a choice between soft and turbulent dreams. People disparage knowing and the intellectual life, and urge doing. I am very content with knowing, if only I could know. That is an august entertainment, and would suffice me a great while. To know a little, would be worth the expense of this world. I hear always the law of Adrastia, "that every soul which had acquired any truth, should be safe from harm until another period."

I know that the world I converse with in the city and in the farms, is not the world I *think*. I observe that difference, and shall observe it. One day, I shall know the value and law of this discrepance. But I have not found that much was gained by manipular attempts to realize the world of thought. Many eager persons successively make an experiment in this way, and make themselves ridiculous. They acquire democratic manners, they foam at the mouth, they hate and deny. Worse, I observe, that, in the history of mankind, there is never a solitary example of success,—taking their own tests of success. I say this polemically, or in reply to the inquiry, why not realize your world? But far be from me the despair which prejudges the law by a paltry empiricism,—since there never was a right endeavor, but it succeeded.

Patience and patience, we shall win at the last. We must be very suspicious of the deceptions of the element of time. It takes a good deal of time to eat or to sleep, or to earn a hundred dollars, and a very little time to entertain a hope and an insight which becomes the light of our life. We dress our garden, eat our dinners, discuss the household with our wives, and these things make no impression, are forgotten next week; but in the solitude to which every man is always returning, he has a sanity and revelations, which in his passage into new worlds he will carry with him. Never mind the ridicule, never mind the defeat: up again, old heart!—it seems to say,—there is victory yet for all justice; and the true romance which the world exists to realize, will be the transformation of genius into practical power.

CHARACTER.

The sun set; but set not his hope:
Stars rose; his faith was earlier up:
Fixed on the enormous galaxy,
Deeper and older seemed his eye:
And matched his sufferance sublime
The taciturnity of time.
He spoke, and words more soft than rain
Brought the Age of Gold again:
His action won such reverence sweet,
As hid all measure of the feat.

(97)

Work of his hand
He nor commends nor grieves:
Pleads for itself the fact;
As unrepenting Nature leaves
Her every act.

(98)

ESSAY III.

CHARACTER.

———

I HAVE read that those who listened to Lord Chatham felt that there was something finer in the man, than anything which he said. It has been complained of our brilliant English historian of the French Revolution, that when he has told all his facts about Mirabeau, they do not justify his estimate of his genius. The Gracchi, Agis, Cleomenes, and others of Plutarch's heroes, do not in the record of facts equal their own fame. Sir Philip Sidney, the Earl of Essex, Sir Walter Raleigh, are men of great figure, and of few deeds. We cannot find the smallest part of the personal weight of Washington, in the narrative of his exploits. The authority of the name of Schiller is too great for his books. This inequality of the reputation to the works or the anecdotes, is not accounted for by saying that the reverberation is longer than the thunder-clap; but somewhat

resided in these men which begot an expectation that outran all their performance. The
largest part of their power was latent. This is
that which we call Character,—a reserved force
which acts directly by presence, and without
means.   It is conceived of as a certain un-
demonstrable force, a Familiar or Genius, by
whose impulses the man is guided, but whose
counsels he cannot impart; which is company
for him, so that such men are often solitary, or
if they chance to be social, do not need society,
but can entertain themselves very well alone.
The purest literary talent appears at one time
great, at another time small, but character is
of a stellar and undiminishable greatness.
What others effect by talent or by eloquence,
this man accomplishes by some magnetism.
"Half his strength he put not forth." His
victories are by demonstration of superiority,
and not by crossing of bayonets. He conquers,
because his arrival alters the face of affairs.
'"O Iole! how did you know that Hercules
was a god?" "Because," answered Iole, "I
was content the moment my eyes fell on him.
When I beheld Theseus, I desired that I might
see him offer battle, or at least guide his horses

in the chariot-race; but Hercules did not wait
for a contest; he conquered whether he stood,
or walked, or sat, or whatever thing he did."
Man, ordinarily a pendant to events, only half
attached, and that awkwardly, to the world he
lives in, in these examples appears to share the
life of things, and to be an expression of the
same laws which control the tides and the sun,
numbers and quantities.

But to use a more modest illustration, and
nearer home, I observe, that in our political
elections, where this element, if it appears at
all, can only occur in its coarsest form, we
sufficiently understand its incomparable rate.
The people know that they need in their representative much more than talent, namely, the
power to make his talent trusted. They cannot
come at their ends by sending to Congress a
learned, acute, and fluent speaker, if he be not
one, who, before he was appointed by the people to represent them, was appointed by Al-
mighty God to stand for a fact,—invincibly
persuaded of that fact in himself,—so that the
most confident and the most violent persons
learn that here is resistance on which both im-
pudence and terror are wasted, namely, faith in

a fact. The men who carry their points do not need to inquire of their constituents what they should say, but are themselves the country which they represent : nowhere are its emotions or opinions so instant and true as in them ; nowhere so pure from a selfish infusion. The constituency at home hearkens to their words, watches the color of their cheek, and therein, as in a glass, dresses its own. Our public assemblies are pretty good tests of manly force. Our frank countrymen of the west and south have a taste for character, and like to know whether the New Englander is a substantial man, or whether the hand can pass through him.

The same motive force appears in trade. There are geniuses in trade, as well as in war, or the state, or letters ; and the reason why this or that man is fortunate, is not to be told. It lies in the man : that is all anybody can tell you about it. See him, and you will know as easily why he succeeds, as, if you see Napoleon, you would comprehend his fortune. In the new objects we recognize the old game, the habit of fronting the fact, and not dealing with it at second hand, through the perceptions of somebody else. Nature seems to authorize trade, as soon as you see the natural merchant, who appears not so much a private agent, as her factor and Minister of Commerce. His natural probity combines with his insight into the fabric of society, to put him above tricks, and he communicates to all his own faith, that contracts are of no private interpretation. The habit of his mind is a reference to standards of natural equity and public advantage; and he inspires respect, and the wish to deal with him, both for the quiet spirit of honor which attends him, and for the intellectual pastime which the spectacle of so much ability affords. This immensely stretched trade, which makes the capes of the Southern Ocean his wharves, and the Atlantic Sea his familiar port, centres in his brain only; and nobody in the universe can make his place good. In his parlor, I see very well that he has been at hard work this morning, with that knitted brow, and that settled humor, which all his desire to be courteous cannot shake off. I see plainly how many firm acts have been done; how many valiant *noes* have this day been spoken, when others would have uttered ruinous *yeas*. I see, with the pride of art, and skill of masterly arithmetic and power of remote combination, the consciousness of being an agent and playfellow of the original laws of the world. He too believes that none can supply him, and that a man must be born to trade, or he cannot learn it.

This virtue draws the mind more, when it appears in action to ends not so mixed. It works with most energy in the smallest companies and in private relations. In all cases, it is an extraordinary and incomputable agent. The excess of physical strength is paralyzed by it. Higher natures overpower lower ones by affecting them with a certain sleep. The faculties are locked up, and offer no resistance. Perhaps that is the universal law. When the high cannot bring up the low to itself, it benumbs it, as man charms down the resistance of the lower animals. Men exert on each other a similar occult power. How often has the influence of a true master realized all the tales of magic! A river of command seemed to run down from his eyes into all those who beheld him, a torrent of strong sad light, like an Ohio or Danube, which pervaded them with his thoughts, and colored all events with the hue

of his mind. " What means did you employ ? "
was the question asked of the wife of Concini, in
regard to her treatment of Mary of Medici ; and
the answer was, " Only that influence which
every strong mind has over a weak one." Cannot Cæsar in irons shuffle off the irons, and
transfer them to the person of Hippo or Thraso
the turnkey? Is an iron handcuff so immuta-
ble a bond? Suppose a slaver on the coast of
Guinea should take on board a gang of negroes,
which should contain persons of the stamp of
Toussaint L'Ouverture : or, let us fancy, under
these swarthy masks he has a gang of Wash-
ingtons in chains. When they arrive at Cuba,
will the relative order of the ship's company be
the same ? Is there nothing but rope and iron?
Is there no love, no reverence ? Is there never
a glimpse of right in a poor slave-captain's
mind ; and cannot these be supposed available
to break, or elude, or in any manner overmatch
the tension of an inch or two of iron ring?

This is a natural power, like light and heat,
and all nature coöperates with it. The reason
why we feel one man's presence, and do not feel
another's, is as simple as gravity. Truth is the
summit of being : justice is the application of it

to affairs. All individual natures stand in a scale, according to the purity of this element in them. The will of the pure runs down from them into other natures, as water runs down from a higher into a lower vessel. This natural force is no more to be withstood, than any other natural force. We can drive a stone upward for a moment into the air, but it is yet true that all stones will forever fall ; and whatever instances can be quoted of unpunished theft, or of a lie which somebody credited, justice must prevail, and it is the privilege of truth to make itself believed. Character is this moral order seen through the medium of an individual nature. An individual is an encloser. Time and space, liberty and necessity, truth and thought, are left at large no longer. Now, the universe is a close or pound. All things exist in the man tinged with the manners of his soul. With what quality is in him, he infuses all nature that he can reach ; nor does he tend to lose himself in vastness, but, at how long a curve soever, all his regards return into his own good at last. He animates all he can, and he sees only what he animates. He encloses the world, as the patriot does his country, as a material basis for his character, and a theatre for action. A healthy soul stands united with the Just and the True, as the magnet arranges itself with the pole, so that he stands to all beholders like a transparent object betwixt them and the sun, and whoso journeys towards the sun, journeys towards that person. He is thus the medium of the highest influence to all who are not on the same level. Thus, men of character are the conscience of the society to which they belong.

The natural measure of this power is the resistance of circumstances. Impure men consider life as it is reflected in opinions, events, and persons. They cannot see the action, until it is done. Yet its moral element pre-existed in the actor, and its quality as right or wrong, it was easy to predict. Everything in nature is bipolar, or has a positive and negative pole. There is a male and a female, a spirit and a fact, a north and a south. Spirit is the positive, the event is the negative. Will is the north, action the south pole. Character may be ranked as having its natural place in the north. It shares the magnetic currents of the system. The feeble souls are drawn to the south or negative pole. They look at the profit or hurt of the action. They never behold a principle until it is lodged in a person. They do not wish to be lovely, but to be loved. The class of character like to hear of their faults; the other class do not like to hear of faults; they worship events; secure to them a fact, a connexion, a certain chain of circumstances, and they will ask no more. The hero sees that the event is ancillary: it must follow *him*. A given order of events has no power to secure to him the satisfaction which the imagination attaches to it; the soul of goodness escapes from any set of circumstances, whilst prosperity belongs to a certain mind, and will introduce that power and victory which is its natural fruit, into any order of events. No change of circumstances can repair a defect of character. We boast our emancipation from many superstitions; but if we have broken any idols, it is through a transfer of the idolatry. What have I gained, that I no longer immolate a bull to Jove, or to Neptune, or a mouse to Hecate; that I do not tremble before the Eu-menides, or the Catholic Purgatory, or the Calvinistic Judgment-day,—if I quake at opin-ion, the public opinion, as we call it; or at the threat of assault, or contumely, or bad neighbors, or poverty, or mutilation, or at the rumor of revolution, or of murder? If I quake, what matters it what I quake at? Our proper vice takes form in one or another shape, according to the sex, age, or temperament of the person, and, if we are capable of fear, will readily find terrors. The covetousness or the malignity which saddens me, when I ascribe it to society, is my own. I am always environed by myself. On the other part, rectitude is a perpetual victory, celebrated not by cries of joy, but by serenity, which is joy fixed or habitual. It is disgraceful to fly to events for confirmation of our truth and worth. The capitalist does not run every hour to the broker, to coin his advantages into current money of the realm; he is satisfied to read in the quotations of the market, that his stocks have risen. The same transport which the occurrence of the best events in the best order would occasion me, I must learn to taste purer in the perception that my position is every hour meliorated, and does already command those events I desire. That exultation is only to be checked by the foresight of an order of things so excellent, as to throw all our prosperities into the deepest shade.

The face which character wears to me is self-sufficingness. I revere the person who is riches; so that I cannot think of him as alone, or poor, or exiled, or unhappy, or a client, but as perpetual patron, benefactor, and beatified man. Character is centrality, the impossibility of being displaced or overset. A man should give us a sense of mass. Society is frivolous, and shreds its day into scraps, its conversation into ceremonies and escapes. But if I go to see an ingenious man, I shall think myself poorly entertained if he give me nimble pieces of benevolence and etiquette; rather he shall stand stoutly in his place, and let me apprehend, if it were only his resistance; know that I have encountered a new and positive quality;—great refreshment for both of us. It is much, that he does not accept the conventional opinions and practices. That nonconformity will remain a goad and remembrancer, and every inquirer will have to dispose of him, in the first place. There is nothing real or useful that is not a seat of war. Our houses ring with laughter and personal and critical gossip, but it helps little. But the uncivil, unavailable man, who is a problem and a threat to society, whom it cannot

let pass in silence, but must either worship or
hate,—and to whom all parties feel related, both
the leaders of opinion, and the obscure and
eccentric,—he helps; he puts America and
Europe in the wrong, and destroys the skepticism which says, 'man is a doll, let us eat and
drink, 'tis the best we can do,' by illuminating
the untried and unknown. Acquiescence in the
establishment, and appeal to the public, indicate
infirm faith, heads which are not clear, and
which must see a house built, before they can
comprehend the plan of it. The wise man not
only leaves out of his thought the many, but
leaves out the few. Fountains, fountains, the
self-moved, the absorbed, the commander because he is commanded, the assured, the primary,—they are good; for these announce the
instant presence of supreme power.

Our action should rest mathematically on
our substance. In nature, there are no false
valuations. A pound of water in the ocean-tem-
pest has no more gravity than in a mid-summer
pond. All things work exactly according to
their quality, and according to their quantity;
attempt nothing they cannot do, except man
only. He has pretension: he wishes and at-

tempts things beyond his force. I read in a
book of English memoirs, "Mr. Fox (afterwards Lord Holland) said, he must have the
Treasury; he had served up to it, and would
have it."—Xenophon and his Ten Thousand
were quite equal to what they attempted, and
did it; so equal, that it was not suspected to
be a grand and inimitable exploit. Yet there
stands that fact unrepeated, a high-water-mark
in military history. Many have attempted it
since, and not been equal to it. It is only on
reality, that any power of action can be based.
No institution will be better than the institutor.
I knew an amiable and accomplished person
who undertook a practical reform, yet I was
never able to find in him the enterprise of love
he took in hand. He adopted it by ear and
by the understanding from the books he had
been reading. All his action was tentative, a
piece of the city carried out into the fields, and
was the city still, and no new fact, and could
not inspire enthusiasm. Had there been something latent in the man, a terrible undemon-
strated genius agitating and embarrassing his
demeanor, we had watched for its advent. It
is not enough that the intellect should see the

evils, and their remedy. We shall still postpone our existence, nor take the ground to
which we are entitled, whilst it is only a thought,
and not a spirit that incites us. We have not
yet served up to it.

These are properties of life, and another trait
is the notice of incessant growth. Men should
be intelligent and earnest. They must also
make us feel, that they have a controlling happy
future, opening before them, which sheds a
splendor on the passing hour. The hero is
misconceived and misreported : he cannot therefore wait to unravel any man's blunders : he is
again on his road, adding new powers and
honors to his domain, and new claims on your
heart, which will bankrupt you, if you have
loitered about the old things, and have not kept
your relation to him, by adding to your wealth.
New actions are the only apologies and explana-
tions of old ones, which the noble can bear to
offer or to receive. If your friend has displeased
you, you shall not sit down to consider it, for
he has already lost all memory of the passage,
and has doubled his power to serve you, and,
ere you can rise up again, will burden you with
blessings.

33

We have no pleasure in thinking of a benevolence that is only measured by its works.
Love is inexhaustible, and if its estate is wasted,
its granary emptied, still cheers and enriches,
and the man, though he sleep, seems to purify
the air, and his house to adorn the landscape
and strengthen the laws. People always recognize this difference. We know who is benevolent, by quite other means than the amount
of subscription to soup-societies. It is only
low merits that can be enumerated. Fear, when
your friends say to you what you have done
well, and say it through ; but when they stand
with uncertain timid looks of respect and half-
dislike, and must suspend their judgment for
years to come, you may begin to hope. Those
who live to the future must always appear selfish
to those who live to the present. Therefore it
was droll in the good Riemer, who has written
memoirs of Goethe, to make out a list of his
donations and good deeds, as, so many hundred
thalers given to Stilling, to Hegel, to Tischbein :
a lucrative place found for Professor Voss, a
post under the Grand Duke for Herder, a
pension for Meyer, two professors recommended
to foreign universities, &c. &c. The longest

list of specifications of benefit, would look very short. A man is a poor creature, if he is to be measured so. For, all these, of course, are exceptions; and the rule and hodiernal life of a good man is benefaction. The true charity of Goethe is to be inferred from the account he gave Dr. Eckermann, of the way in which he had spent his fortune. "Each bon-mot of mine has cost a purse of gold. Half a million of my own money, the fortune I inherited, my salary, and the large income derived from my writings for fifty years back, have been expended to instruct me in what I now know. I have besides seen," &c.

I own it is but poor chat and gossip to go to enumerate traits of this simple and rapid power, and we are painting the lightning with charcoal; but in these long nights and vacations, I like to console myself so. Nothing but itself can copy it. A word warm from the heart enriches me. I surrender at discretion. How death-cold is literary genius before this fire of life! These are the touches that reanimate my heavy soul, and give it eyes to pierce the dark of nature. I find, where I thought myself poor, there was I most rich. Thence comes a new intellectual

exaltation, to be again rebuked by some new
exhibition of character. Strange alternation of
attraction and repulsion! Character repudiates
intellect, yet excites it; and character passes
into thought, is published so, and then is
ashamed before new flashes of moral worth.

Character is nature in the highest form. It
is of no use to ape it, or to contend with it.
Somewhat is possible of resistance, and of per-
sistence, and of creation, to this power, which
will foil all emulation.

This masterpiece is best where no hands but
nature's have been laid on it. Care is taken
that the greatly-destined shall slip up into life
in the shade, with no thousand-eyed Athens to
watch and blazon every new thought, every
blushing emotion of young genius. Two persons lately,—very young children of the most
high God,—have given me occasion for thought.
When I explored the source of their sanctity,
and charm for the imagination, it seemed as if
each answered, ' From my non-conformity: I
never listened to your people's law, or to what
they call their gospel, and wasted my time. I
was content with the simple rural poverty of
my own: hence this sweetness: my work never

reminds you of that;—is pure of that.' And
nature advertises me in such persons, that, in
democratic America, she will not be demo-
cratized. How cloistered and constitutionally
sequestered from the market and from scandal!
It was only this morning, that I sent away some
wild flowers of these wood-gods. They are a
relief from literature,—these fresh draughts from
the sources of thought and sentiment; as we
read, in an age of polish and criticism, the first
lines of written prose and verse of a nation.
How captivating is their devotion to their favorite books, whether Æschylus, Dante, Shakspeare, or Scott, as feeling that they have a
stake in that book: who touches that, touches
them;—and especially the total solitude of the
critic, the Patmos of thought from which he
writes, in unconsciousness of any eyes that shall
ever read this writing. Could they dream on
still, as angels, and not wake to comparisons,
and to be flattered! Yet some natures are too
good to be spoiled by praise, and wherever the
vein of thought reaches down into the profound, there is no danger from vanity. Solemn
friends will warn them of the danger of the
head's being turned by the flourish of trumpets,

but they can afford to smile. I remember the indignation of an eloquent Methodist at the kind admonitions of a Doctor of Divinity,—' My friend, a man can neither be praised nor insulted.' But forgive the counsels; they are very natural. I remember the thought which occurred to me when some ingenious and spiritual foreigners came to America, was, Have you been victimized in being brought hither?—or, prior to that, answer me this, ' Are you victimizable ? '

As I have said, nature keeps these sovereignties in her own hands, and however pertly our sermons and disciplines would divide some share of credit, and teach that the laws fashion the citizen, she goes her own gait, and puts the wisest in the wrong. She makes very light of gospels and prophets, as one who has a great many more to produce, and no excess of time to spare on any one. There is a class of men, individuals of which appear at long intervals, so eminently endowed with insight and virtue, that they have been unanimously saluted as *divine*, and who seem to be an accumulation of that power we consider. Divine persons are character born, or, to borrow a phrase from Napo-

leon, they are victory organized. They are
usually received with ill-will, because they are
new, and because they set a bound to the exaggeration that has been made of the personality of the last divine person. Nature never
rhymes her children, nor makes two men alike.
When we see a great man, we fancy a resem-
blance to some historical person, and predict
the sequel of his character and fortune, a result
which he is sure to disappoint. None will ever
solve the problem of his character according to
our prejudice, but only in his own high un-
precedented way. Character wants room; must
not be crowded on by persons, nor be judged
from glimpses got in the press of affairs or on
few occasions. It needs perspective, as a great
building. It may not, probably does not, form
relations rapidly; and we should not require
rash explanation, either on the popular ethics,
or on our own, of its action.

I look on Sculpture as history. I do not
think the Apollo and the Jove impossible in
flesh and blood. Every trait which the artist
recorded in stone, he had seen in life, and better
than his copy. We have seen many counter-
feits, but we are born believers in great men.

How easily we read in old books, when men
were few, of the smallest action of the patriarchs.
We require that a man should be so large and
columnar in the landscape, that it should de-
serve to be recorded, that he arose, and girded
up his loins, and departed to such a place.   The
most credible pictures are those of majestic men
who prevailed at their entrance, and convinced
the senses; as happened to the eastern magian
who was sent to test the merits of Zertusht or
Zoroaster.   When the Yunani sage arrived at
Balkh, the Persians tell us, Gushtasp appointed
a day on which the Mobeds of every country
should assemble, and a golden chair was placed
for the Yunani sage.   Then the beloved of Yez-
dam, the prophet Zertusht, advanced into the
midst of the assembly.   The Yunani sage, on
seeing that chief, said, "This form and this gait
cannot lie, and nothing but truth can proceed
from them."   Plato said, it was impossible not
to believe in the children of the gods, "though
they should speak without probable or necessary arguments."   I should think myself very
unhappy in my associates, if I could not credit
the best things in history.   "John Bradshaw,"
says Milton, "appears like a consul, from whom

the fasces are not to depart with the year; so that not on the tribunal only, but throughout his life, you would regard him as sitting in judgment upon kings." I find it more credible, since it is anterior information, that one man should *know heaven*, as the Chinese say, than that so many men should know the world. " The virtuous prince confronts the gods, without any misgiving. He waits a hundred ages till a sage comes, and does not doubt. He who confronts the gods, without any misgiving, knows heaven; he who waits a hundred ages until a sage comes, without doubting, knows men. Hence the virtuous prince moves, and for ages shows empire the way." But there is no need to seek remote examples. He is a dull observer whose experience has not taught him the reality and force of magic, as well as of chemistry. The coldest precisian cannot go abroad without encountering inexplicable influences. One man fastens an eye on him, and the graves of the memory render up their dead; the secrets that make him wretched either to keep or to betray, must be yielded;—another, and he cannot speak, and the bones of his body seem to lose their cartilages; the entrance of a friend adds grace, boldness, and eloquence to him; and there are persons, he cannot choose but remember, who gave a transcendant expansion to his thought, and kindled another life in his bosom.

What is so excellent as strict relations of amity, when they spring from this deep root? The sufficient reply to the skeptic, who doubts the power and the furniture of man, is in that possibility of joyful intercourse with persons, which makes the faith and practice of all reasonable men. I know nothing which life has to offer so satisfying as the profound good understanding, which can subsist, after much exchange of good offices, between two virtuous men, each of whom is sure of himself, and sure of his friend. It is a happiness which postpones all other gratifications, and makes politics, and commerce, and churches, cheap. For, when men shall meet as they ought, each a benefactor, a shower of stars, clothed with thoughts, with deeds, with accomplishments, it should be the festival of nature which all things announce. Of such friendship, love in the sexes is the first symbol, as all other things are symbols of love. Those relations to the best men, which, at one time, we reckoned the romances of youth, become, in the progress of the character, the most solid enjoyment.

If it were possible to live in right relations with men!—if we could abstain from asking anything of them, from asking their praise, or help, or pity, and content us with compelling them through the virtue of the eldest laws! Could we not deal with a few persons,—with one person,—after the unwritten statutes, and make an experiment of their efficacy? Could we not pay our friend the compliment of truth, of silence, of forbearing? Need we be so eager to seek him? If we are related, we shall meet. It was a tradition of the ancient world, that no metamorphosis could hide a god from a god; and there is a Greek verse which runs,

> " The Gods are to each other not unknown."

Friends also follow the laws of divine necessity; they gravitate to each other, and cannot otherwise :—

> When each the other shall avoid,
> Shall each by each be most enjoyed.

Their relation is not made, but allowed. The gods must seat themselves without seneschal in

our Olympus, and as they can instal themselves
by seniority divine.   Society is spoiled, if pains
are taken, if the associates are brought a mile
to meet.   And if it be not society, it is a mis-
chievous, low, degrading jangle, though made
up of the best.   All the greatness of each is
kept back, and every foible in painful activity,
as if the Olympians should meet to exchange
snuff-boxes.

Life goes headlong.   We chase some flying
scheme, or we are hunted by some fear or command behind us.   But if suddenly we encounter
a friend, we pause; our heat and hurry look
foolish enough; now pause, now possession, is
required, and the power to swell the moment
from the resources of the heart.   The moment
is all, in all noble relations.

A divine person is the prophecy of the mind;
a friend is the hope of the heart.   Our beatitude
waits for the fulfilment of these two in one.
The ages are opening this moral force.   All
force is the shadow or symbol of that.   Poetry
is joyful and strong, as it draws its inspiration
thence.   Men write their names on the world,
as they are filled with this.   History has been
mean ; our nations have been mobs; we have .

never seen a man : that divine form we do not yet know, but only the dream and prophecy of such : we do not know the majestic manners which belong to him, which appease and exalt the beholder. We shall one day see that the most private is the most public energy, that quality atones for quantity, and grandeur of character acts in the dark, and succors them who never saw it. What greatness has yet appeared, is beginnings and encouragements to us in this direction. The history of those gods and saints which the world has written, and then worshipped, are documents of character. The ages have exulted in the manners of a youth who owed nothing to fortune, and who was hanged at the Tyburn of his nation, who, by the pure quality of his nature, shed an epic splendor around the facts of his death, which has transfigured every particular into an universal symbol for the eyes of mankind. This great defeat is hitherto our highest fact. But the mind requires a victory to the senses, a force of character which will convert judge, jury, soldier, and king ; which will rule animal and mineral virtues, and blend with the courses of sap, of rivers, of winds, of stars, and of moral agents.

If we cannot attain at a bound to these grandeurs, at least, let us do them homage. In society, high advantages are set down to the possessor, as disadvantages. It requires the more wariness in our private estimates. I do not forgive in my friends the failure to know a fine character, and to entertain it with thankful hospitality. When, at last, that which we have always longed for, is arrived, and shines on us with glad rays out of that far celestial land, then to be coarse, then to be critical, and treat such a visitant with the jabber and suspicion of the streets, argues a vulgarity that seems to shut the doors of heaven. This is confusion, this the right insanity, when the soul no longer knows its own, nor where its allegiance, its religion, are due. Is there any religion but this, to know, that, wherever in the wide desert of being, the holy sentiment we cherish has opened into a flower, it blooms for me? if none sees it, I see it; I am aware, if I alone, of the greatness of the fact. Whilst it blooms, I will keep sabbath or holy time, and suspend my gloom, and my folly and jokes. Nature is indulged by the presence of this guest. There are many eyes that can detect and honor the

prudent and household virtues; there are many
that can discern Genius on his starry track,
though the mob is incapable; but when that
love which is all-suffering, all-abstaining, all-
aspiring, which has vowed to itself, that it will
be a wretch and also a fool in this world, sooner
than soil its white hands by any compliances,
comes into our streets and houses,—only the
pure and aspiring can know its face, and the
only compliment they can pay it, is to own it.

MANNERS.

" How near to good is what is fair !
  Which we no sooner see,
  But with the lines and outward air
  Our senses taken be.

  Again yourselves compose,
  And now put all the aptness on
  Of Figure, that Proportion
    Or Color can disclose;
  That if those silent arts were lost,
  Design and Picture, they might boast
    From you a newer ground,
  Instructed by the heightening sense
  Of dignity and reverence
    In their true motions found."

BEN JONSON.

(129)

شب

ESSAY IV.

MANNERS.

———

HALF the world, it is said, knows not how the other half live. Our Exploring Expedition saw the Feejee islanders getting their dinner off human bones; and they are said to eat their own wives and children. The husbandry of the modern inhabitants of Gournou (west of old Thebes) is philosophical to a fault. To set up their housekeeping, nothing is requisite but two or three earthern pots, a stone to grind meal, and a mat which is the bed. The house, namely, a tomb, is ready without rent or taxes. No rain can pass through the roof, and there is no door, for there is no want of one, as there is nothing to lose. If the house do not please them, they walk out and enter another, as there are several hundreds at their command. "It is somewhat singular," adds Belzoni, to whom we owe this account, "to talk of happiness among people who live in sepulchres, among the corpses and rags of an ancient nation which they know nothing of." In the deserts of Borgoo, the rock-Tibboos still dwell in caves, like cliff-swallows, and the language of these negroes is compared by their neighbors to the shrieking of bats, and to the whistling of birds. Again, the Bornoos have no proper names ; individuals are called after their height, thickness, or other accidental quality, and have nicknames merely. But the salt, the dates, the ivory, and the gold, for which these horrible regions are visited, find their way into countries, where the purchaser and consumer can hardly be ranked in one race with these cannibals and man-stealers ; countries where man serves himself with metals, wood, stone, glass, gum, cotton, silk, and wool ; honors himself with architecture ; writes laws, and contrives to execute his will through the hands of many nations ; and, especially, establishes a select society, running through all the countries of intelligent men, a self-constituted aristocracy, or fraternity of the best, which, without written law or exact usage of any kind, perpetuates itself, colonizes every new-planted island, and adopts and makes its own whatever personal beauty or extraordinary native endowment anywhere appears.

What fact more conspicuous in modern history, than the creation of the gentleman? Chivalry is that, and loyalty is that, and, in English literature, half the drama, and all the novels, from Sir Philip Sidney to Sir Walter Scott, paint this figure. The word *gentleman*, which, like the word Christian, must hereafter characterize the present and the few preceding centuries, by the importance attached to it, is a homage to personal and incommunicable properties. Frivolous and fantastic additions have got associated with the name, but the steady interest of mankind in it must be attributed to the valuable properties which it designates. An element which unites all the most forcible persons of every country; makes them intelligible and agreeable to each other, and is somewhat so precise, that it is at once felt if an individual lack the masonic sign, cannot be any casual product, but must be an average result of the character and faculties universally found in men. It seems a certain permanent average; as the atmosphere is a permanent composition, whilst so many gases are combined only to be decompounded. *Comme il faut*, is the Frenchman's description of good society, *as we must be*. It is a spontaneous fruit of talents and feelings of precisely that class who have most vigor, who take the lead in the world of this hour, and, though far from pure, far from constituting the gladdest and highest tone of human feeling, is as good as the whole society permits it to be. It is made of the spirit, more than of the talent of men, and is a compound result, into which every great force enters as an ingredient, namely, virtue, wit, beauty, wealth, and power.

There is something equivocal in all the words in use to express the excellence of manners and social cultivation, because the quantities are fluxional, and the last effect is assumed by the senses as the cause. The word *gentleman* has not any correlative abstract to express the quality. *Gentility* is mean, and *gentilesse* is obsolete. But we must keep alive in the vernacular, the distinction between *fashion*, a word of narrow and often sinister meaning, and the heroic character which the gentleman imports. The usual words, however, must be respected: they will be found to contain the root of the matter. The point of distinction in all this class of names, as courtesy, chivalry, fashion, and the like, is, that the flower and fruit, not the grain

of the tree, are contemplated. It is beauty
which is the aim this time, and not worth. The
result is now in question, although our words
intimate well enough the popular feeling, that
the appearance supposes a substance. The gentleman is a man of truth, lord of his own actions,
and expressing that lordship in his behavior,
not in any manner dependent and servile either
on persons, or opinions, or possessions. Beyond this fact of truth and real force, the word
denotes good-nature or benevolence: manhood
first, and then gentleness. The popular notion
certainly adds a condition of ease and fortune;
but that is a natural result of personal force and
love, that they should possess and dispense the
goods of the world. In times of violence, every
eminent person must fall in with many opportuni-
ties to approve his stoutness and worth; therefore every man's name that emerged at all from
the mass in the feudal ages, rattles in our ear
like a flourish of trumpets. But personal force
never goes out of fashion. That is still paramount today, and, in the moving crowd of good
society, the men of valor and reality are known,
and rise to their natural place. The competition is transferred from war to politics and

trade, but the personal force appears readily enough in these new arenas.

Power first, or no leading class. In politics and in trade, bruisers and pirates are of better promise than talkers and clerks. God knows that all sorts of gentlemen knock at the door; but whenever used in strictness, and with any emphasis, the name will be found to point at original energy. It describes a man standing in his own right, and working after untaught methods. In a good lord, there must first be a good animal, at least to the extent of yielding the incomparable advantage of animal spirits. The ruling class must have more, but they must have these, giving in every company the sense of power, which makes things easy to be done which daunt the wise. The society of the energetic class, in their friendly and festive meetings, is full of courage, and of attempts, which intimidate the pale scholar. The courage which girls exhibit is like a battle of Lundy's Lane, or a sea-fight. The intellect relies on memory to make some supplies to face these extemporaneous squadrons. But memory is a base mendicant with basket and badge, in the presence of these sudden masters. The rulers of society must be up to the work of the world, and equal to their versatile office: men of the right Cæsarian pattern, who have great range of affinity. I am far from believing the timid maxim of Lord Falkland, ("that for ceremony there must go two to it; since a bold fellow will go through the cunningest forms,") and am of opinion that the gentleman is the bold fellow whose forms are not to be broken through; and only that plenteous nature is rightful master, which is the complement of whatever person it converses with. My gentleman gives the law where he is; he will outpray saints in chapel, outgeneral veterans in the field, and outshine all courtesy in the hall. He is good company for pirates, and good with academicians; so that it is useless to fortify yourself against him; he has the private entrance to all minds, and I could as easily exclude myself, as him. The famous gentlemen of Asia and Europe have been of this strong type: Saladin, Sapor, the Cid, Julius Cæsar, Scipio, Alexander, Pericles, and the lordliest personages. They sat very carelessly in their chairs, and were too excellent themselves, to value any condition at a high rate.

A plentiful fortune is reckoned necessary, in

the popular judgment, to the completion of this man of the world: and it is a material deputy which walks through the dance which the first has led.   Money is not essential, but this wide affinity is, which transcends the habits of clique and caste, and makes itself felt by men of all classes.   If the aristocrat is only valid in fashionable circles, and not with truckmen, he will never be a leader in fashion ; and if the man of the people cannot speak on equal terms with the gentleman, so that the gentleman shall perceive that he is already really of his own order, he is not to be feared.   Diogenes, Socrates, and Epaminondas, are gentlemen of the best blood, who have chosen the condition of poverty, when that of wealth was equally open to them.   I use these old names, but the men I speak of are my contemporaries.   Fortune will not supply to every generation one of these well-appointed knights, but every collection of men furnishes some example of the class : and the politics of this country, and the trade of every town, are controlled by these hardy and irresponsible doers, who have invention to take the lead, and a broad sympathy which puts them in fellowship with crowds, and makes their action popular.

The manners of this class are observed and caught with devotion by men of taste. The association of these masters with each other, and with men intelligent of their merits, is mutually agreeable and stimulating. The good forms, the happiest expressions of each, are repeated and adopted. By swift consent, everything superfluous is dropped, everything graceful is renewed. Fine manners show themselves formidable to the uncultivated man. They are a subtler science of defence to parry and intimidate ; but once matched by the skill of the other party, they drop the point of the sword,— points and fences disappear, and the youth finds himself in a more transparent atmosphere, wherein life is a less troublesome game, and not a misunderstanding rises between the players. Manners aim to facilitate life, to get rid of impediments, and bring the man pure to energize. They aid our dealing and conversation, as a railway aids travelling, by getting rid of all avoidable obstructions of the road, and leaving nothing to be conquered but pure space. These forms very soon become fixed, and a fine sense of propriety is cultivated with the more heed, that it becomes a badge of social and civil dis-

tinctions. Thus grows up Fashion, an equivocal semblance, the most puissant, the most
fantastic and frivolous, the most feared and
followed, and which morals and violence assault
in vain.

There exists a strict relation between the
class of power, and the exclusive and polished
circles. The last are always filled or filling
from the first. The strong men usually give
some allowance even to the petulances of
fashion, for that affinity they find in it. Napoleon, child of the revolution, destroyer of the
old noblesse, never ceased to court the Fau-
bourg St. Germain: doubtless with the feeling,
that fashion is a homage to men of his stamp.
Fashion, though in a strange way, represents
all manly virtue. It is virtue gone to seed: it
is a kind of posthumous honor. It does not
often caress the great, but the children of the
great: it is a hall of the Past. It usually sets
its face against the great of this hour. Great
men are not commonly in its halls: they are
absent in the field: they are working, not tri-
umphing. Fashion is made up of their children; of those, who, through the value and
virtue of somebody, have acquired lustre to

their name, marks of distinction, means of
cultivation and generosity, and, in their physical
organization, a certain health and excellence,
which secures to them, if not the highest power
to work, yet high power to enjoy. The class
of power, the working heroes, the Cortez, the
Nelson, the Napoleon, see that this is the festivity and permanent celebration of such as
they; that fashion is funded talent; is Mexico,
Marengo, and Trafalgar beaten out thin; that
the brilliant names of fashion run back to just
such busy names as their own, fifty or sixty
years ago. They are the sowers, their sons
shall be the reapers, and *their* sons, in the ordinary course of things, must yield the possession of the harvest to new competitors with
keener eyes and stronger frames. The city is
recruited from the country. In the year 1805,
it is said, every legitimate monarch in Europe
was imbecile. The city would have died out,
rotted, and exploded, long ago, but that it was
reinforced from the fields. It is only country
which came to town day before yesterday, that
is city and court to-day.

Aristocracy and fashion are certain inevitable
results. These mutual selections are indestruc-

tible.   If they provoke anger in the least fa-
vored class, and the excluded majority revenge
themselves on the excluding minority, by the
strong hand, and kill them, at once a new class
finds itself at the top, as certainly as cream rises
in a bowl of milk : and if the people should de-
troy class after class, until two men only were
left, one of these would be the leader, and would
be involuntarily served and copied by the other.
You may keep this minority out of sight and
out of mind, but it is tenacious of life, and is
one of the estates of the realm.   I am the more
struck with this tenacity, when I see its work.
It respects the administration of such unimpor-
tant matters, that we should not look for any
durability in its rule.   We sometimes meet men
under some strong moral influence, as, a patri-
otic, a literary, a religious movement, and feel
that the moral sentiment rules man and nature.
We think all other distinctions and ties will be
slight and fugitive, this of caste or fashion, for
example ; yet come from year to year, and see
how permanent that is, in this Boston or New
York life of man, where, too, it has not the
least countenance from the law of the land.
Not in Egypt or in India a firmer or more im-

passable line. Here are associations whose
ties go over, and under, and through it, a meeting of merchants, a military corps, a college-
class, a fire-club, a professional association, a
political, a religious convention;—the persons
seem to draw inseparably near; yet, that assembly once dispersed, its members will not in the
year meet again. Each returns to his degree
in the scale of good society, porcelain remains
porcelain, and earthen earthen. The objects
of fashion may be frivolous, or fashion may
be objectless, but the nature of this union and
selection can be neither frivolous nor accidental. Each man's rank in that perfect grad-
uation depends on some symmetry in his structure, or some agreement in his structure to the
symmetry of society. Its doors unbar instan-
taneously to a natural claim of their own kind.
A natural gentleman finds his way in, and will
keep the oldest patrician out, who has lost his
intrinsic rank. Fashion understands itself;
good-breeding and personal superiority of whatever country readily fraternize with those of
every other. The chiefs of savage tribes have
distinguished themselves in London and Paris,
by the purity of their tournure.

To say what good of fashion we can,—it rests on reality, and hates nothing so much as pretenders;—to exclude and mystify pretenders, and send them into everlasting 'Coventry,' is its delight. We contemn, in turn, every other gift of men of the world; but the habit even in little and the least matters, of not appealing to any but our own sense of propriety, constitutes the foundation of all chivalry. There is almost no kind of self-reliance, so it be sane and proportioned, which fashion does not occasionally adopt, and give it the freedom of its saloons. A sainted soul is always elegant, and, if it will, passes unchallenged into the most guarded ring. But so will Jock the teamster pass, in some crisis that brings him thither, and find favor, as long as his head is not giddy with the new circumstance, and the iron shoes do not wish to dance in waltzes and cotillons. For there is nothing settled in manners, but the laws of behavior yield to the energy of the individual. The maiden at her first ball, the countryman at a city dinner, believes that there is a ritual according to which every act and compliment must be performed, or the failing party must be cast out of this presence. Later,

they learn that good sense and character make
their own forms every moment, and speak or
abstain, take wine or refuse it, stay or go, sit
in a chair or sprawl with children on the floor,
or stand on their head, or what else soever, in
a new and aboriginal way : and that strong will
is always in fashion, let who will be unfashionable. All that fashion demands is composure,
and self-content. A circle of men perfectly
well-bred would be a company of sensible persons, in which every man's native manners and
character appeared. If the fashionist have not
this quality, he is nothing. We are such lovers
of self-reliance, that we excuse in a man many
sins, if he will show us a complete satisfaction
in his position, which asks no leave to be, of
mine, or any man's good opinion. But any deference to some eminent man or woman of the
world, forfeits all privilege of nobility. He is
an underling : I have nothing to do with him ;
I will speak with his master. A man should
not go where he cannot carry his whole sphere
or society with him,—not bodily, the whole
circle of his friends, but atmospherically. He
should preserve in a new company the same
attitude of mind and reality of relation, which
35

his daily associates draw him to, else he is shorn of his best beams, and will be an orphan in the merriest club. "If you could see Vich Ian Vohr with his tail on!——" But Vich Ian Vohr must always carry his belongings in some fashion, if not added as honor, then severed as disgrace.

There will always be in society certain persons who are mercuries of its approbation, and whose glance will at any time determine for the curious their standing in the world. These are the chamberlains of the lesser gods. Accept their coldness as an omen of grace with the loftier deities, and allow them all their privilege. They are clear in their office, nor could they be thus formidable, without their own merits. But do not measure the importance of this class by their pretension, or imagine that a fop can be the dispenser of honor and shame. They pass also at their just rate; for how can they otherwise, in circles which exist as a sort of herald's office for the sifting of character?

As the first thing man requires of man, is reality, so, that appears in all the forms of society. We pointedly, and by name, introduce the parties to each other. Know you before all heaven and earth, that this is Andrew, and this is Gregory;—they look each other in the eye; they grasp each other's hand, to identify and signalize each other. It is a great satisfaction. A gentleman never dodges: his eyes look straight forward, and he assures the other party, first of all, that he has been met. For what is it that we seek, in so many visits and hospitalities? Is it your draperies, pictures, and decorations? Or, do we not insatiably ask, Was a man in the house? I may easily go into a great household where there is much substance, excellent provision for comfort, luxury, and taste, and yet not encounter there any Amphitryon, who shall subordinate these appendages. I may go into a cottage, and find a farmer who feels that he is the man I have come to see, and fronts me accordingly. It was therefore a very natural point of old feudal etiquette, that a gentleman who received a visit, though it were of his sovereign, should not leave his roof, but should wait his arrival at the door of his house. No house, though it were the Tuileries, or the Escurial, is good for anything without a master. And yet we are not often gratified by this hospitality.

Every body we know surrounds himself with a
fine house, fine books, conservatory, gardens,
equipage, and all manner of toys, as screens to
interpose between himself and his guest. Does
it not seem as if man was of a very sly, elusive
nature, and dreaded nothing so much as a full
rencontre front to front with his fellow? It
were unmerciful, I know, quite to abolish the
use of these screens, which are of eminent convenience, whether the guest is too great, or too
little. We call together many friends who
keep each other in play, or, by luxuries and
ornaments we amuse the young people, and
guard our retirement. Or if, perchance, a
searching realist comes to our gate, before whose
eye we have no care to stand, then again we
run to our curtain, and hide ourselves as Adam
at the voice of the Lord God in the garden.
Cardinal Caprara, the Pope's legate at Paris,
defended himself from the glances of Napoleon,
by an immense pair of green spectacles. Napoleon remarked them, and speedily managed to
rally them off: and yet Napoleon, in his turn,
was not great enough with eight hundred thousand troops at his back, to face a pair of free-
born eyes, but fenced himself with etiquette,

and within triple barriers of reserve: and, as all the world knows from Madame de Stael, was wont, when he found himself observed, to discharge his face of all expression. But emperors and rich men are by no means the most skilful masters of good manners. No rentroll nor army-list can dignify skulking and dissimulation: and the first point of courtesy must always be truth, as really all the forms of good-breeding point that way.

I have just been reading, in Mr. Hazlitt's translation, Montaigne's account of his journey into Italy, and am struck with nothing more agreeably than the self-respecting fashions of the time. His arrival in each place, the arrival of a gentleman of France, is an event of some consequence. Wherever he goes, he pays a visit to whatever prince or gentleman of note resides upon his road, as a duty to himself and to civilization. When he leaves any house in which he has lodged for a few weeks, he causes his arms to be painted and hung up as a perpetual sign to the house as was the custom of gentlemen.

The complement of this graceful self-respect, and that of all the points of good breeding I most require and insist upon, is deference. I like that every chair should be a throne, and hold a king. I prefer a tendency to stateliness, to an excess of fellowship. Let the incommunicable objects of nature and the metaphysical isolation of man teach us independence. Let us not be too much acquainted. I would have a man enter his house through a hall filled with heroic and sacred sculptures, that he might not want the hint of tranquillity and self-poise. We should meet each morning, as from foreign countries, and spending the day together, should depart at night, as into foreign countries. In all things I would have the island of a man inviolate. Let us sit apart as the gods, talking from peak to peak all round Olympus. No degree of affection need invade this religion. This is myrrh and rosemary to keep the other sweet. Lovers should guard their strangeness. If they forgive too much, all slides into confusion and meanness. It is easy to push this deference to a Chinese etiquette; but coolness and absence of heat and haste indicate fine qualities. A gentleman makes no noise: a lady is serene. Proportionate is our disgust at those invaders who fill a studious house with blast

and running, to secure some paltry convenience.
Not less I dislike a low sympathy of each with
his neighbor's needs.   Must we have a good understanding with one another's palates? as foolish people who have lived long together, know
when each wants salt or sugar.   I pray my
companion, if he wishes for bread, to ask me
for bread, and if he wishes for sassafras or
arsenic, to ask me for them, and not to hold out
his plate, as if I knew already.   Every natural
function can be dignified by deliberation and
privacy.   Let us leave hurry to slaves.   The
compliments and ceremonies of our breeding
should signify, however remotely, the recollection of the grandeur of our destiny.

The flower of courtesy does not very well
bide handling, but if we dare to open another
leaf, and explore what parts go to its confor-
mation, we shall find also an intellectual quality.   To the leaders of men, the brain as well as
the flesh and the heart must furnish a proportion.   Defect in manners is usually the defect
of fine perceptions.   Men are too coarsely made
for the delicacy of beautiful carriage and customs.   It is not quite sufficient to good-breeding, a union of kindness and independence.

We imperatively require a perception of, and a homage to beauty in our companions. Other virtues are in request in the field and workyard, but a certain degree of taste is not to be spared in those we sit with. I could better eat with one who did not respect the truth or the laws, than with a sloven and unpresentable person. Moral qualities rule the world, but at short distances, the senses are despotic. The same discrimination of fit and fair runs out, if with less rigor, into all parts of life. The average spirit of the energetic class is good sense, acting under certain limitations and to certain ends. It entertains every natural gift. Social in its nature, it respects everything which tends to unite men. It delights in measure. The love of beauty is mainly the love of measure or proportion. The person who screams, or uses the superlative degree, or converses with heat, puts whole drawing-rooms to flight. If you wish to be loved, love measure. You must have genius, or a prodigious usefulness, if you will hide the want of measure. This perception comes in to polish and perfect the parts of the social instrument. Society will pardon much to genius and special gifts, but, being in its nature a convention, it loves what is conventional, or what belongs to coming together. That makes the good and bad of manners, namely, what helps or hinders fellowship. For, fashion is not good sense absolute, but relative; not good sense private, but good sense entertaining company. It hates corners and sharp points of character, hates quarrelsome, egotistical, solitary, and gloomy people; hates whatever can interfere with total blending of parties; whilst it values all peculiarities as in the highest degree refreshing, which can consist with good fellowship. And besides the general infusion of wit to heighten civility, the direct splendor of intellectual power is ever welcome in fine society as the costliest addition to its rule and its credit.

The dry light must shine in to adorn our festival, but it must be tempered and shaded, or that will also offend. Accuracy is essential to beauty, and quick perceptions to politeness, but not too quick perceptions. One may be too punctual and too precise. He must leave the omniscience of business at the door, when he comes into the palace of beauty. Society loves creole natures, and sleepy, languishing manners, so that they cover sense, grace, and good-will; the air of drowsy strength, which disarms criticism; perhaps, because such a person seems to reserve himself for the best of the game, and not spend himself on surfaces; an ignoring eye, which does not see the annoyances, shifts, and inconveniences, that cloud the brow and smother the voice of the sensitive.

Therefore, besides personal force and so much perception as constitutes unerring taste, society demands in its patrician class, another element already intimated, which it significantly terms good-nature, expressing all degrees of generosity, from the lowest willingness and faculty to oblige, up to the heights of magnanimity and love. Insight we must have, or we shall run against one another, and miss the way to our food; but intellect is selfish and barren. The secret of success in society, is a certain heartiness and sympathy. A man who is not happy in the company, cannot find any word in his memory that will fit the occasion. All his information is a little impertinent. A man who is happy there, finds in every turn of the conversation equally lucky occasions for the introduction of that which he has to say. The favorites of society, and what it calls *whole souls*, are able men, and of more spirit than wit, who have no uncomfortable egotism, but who exactly fill the hour and the company, contented and contenting, at a marriage or a funeral, a ball or a jury, a water-party or a shooting-match. England, which is rich in gentlemen, furnished, in the beginning of the present century, a good model of that genius which the world loves, in Mr. Fox, who added to his great abilities the most social disposition, and real love of men. Parliamentary history has few better passages than the debate, in which Burke and Fox separated in the House of Commons; when Fox urged on his old friend the claims of old friendship with such tenderness, that the house was moved to tears. Another anecdote is so close to my matter, that I must hazard the story. A tradesman who had long dunned him for a note of three hundred guineas, found him one day counting gold, and demanded payment: " No," said Fox, " I owe this money to Sheridan : it is a debt of honor: if an accident should happen to me, he has nothing to show." " Then," said the creditor, " I change my debt into a debt of honor," and tore the note in pieces. Fox thanked the man for his confidence, and paid him, saying, "his debt was of older standing, and Sheridan must wait." Lover of liberty, friend of the Hindoo, friend of the African slave, he possessed a great personal popularity; and Napoleon said of him on the occasion of his visit to Paris, in 1805, "Mr. Fox will always hold the first place in an assembly at the Tuileries."

We may easily seem ridiculous in our eulogy of courtesy, whenever we insist on benevolence as its foundation. The painted phantasm Fashion rises to cast a species of derision on what we say. But I will neither be driven from some allowance to Fashion as a symbolic institution, nor from the belief that love is the basis of courtesy. We must obtain *that*, if we can; but by all means we must affirm *this*. Life owes much of its spirit to these sharp contrasts. Fashion which affects to be honor, is often, in all men's experience, only a ballroom-code. Yet, so long as it is the highest circle, in the imagination of the best heads on the planet, there is something necessary and excellent in it; for it is not to be supposed that men have agreed to be the dupes of anything preposterous; and the

respect which these mysteries inspire in the
most rude and sylvan characters, and the curi-
osity with which details of high life are read,
betray the universality of the love of cultivated
manners. I know that a comic disparity would
be felt, if we should enter the acknowledged
'first circles,' and apply these terrific standards
of justice, beauty, and benefit, to the individuals
actually found there. Monarchs and heroes,
sages and lovers, these gallants are not. Fashion has many classes and many rules of probation and admission; and not the best alone.
There is not only the right of conquest, which
genius pretends,—the individual, demonstrat-
ing his natural aristocracy best of the best;
—but less claims will pass for the time; for
Fashion loves lions, and points, like Circe, to
her horned company. This gentleman is this
afternoon arrived from Denmark; and that is
my Lord Ride, who came yesterday from
Bagdat; here is Captain Friese, from Cape
Turnagain; and Captain Symmes, from the
interior of the earth; and Monsieur Jovaire,
who came down this morning in a balloon;
Mr. Hobnail, the reformer; and Reverend Jul
Bat, who has converted the whole torrid zone

in his Sunday school; and Signor Torre del Greco, who extinguished Vesuvius by pouring into it the Bay of Naples; Spahi, the Persian ambassador; and Tul Wil Shan, the exiled nabob of Nepaul, whose saddle is the new moon. —But these are monsters of one day, and to-morrow will be dismissed to their holes and dens; for, in these rooms, every chair is waited for. The artist, the scholar, and, in general, the clerisy, wins its way up into these places, and gets represented here, somewhat on this footing of conquest. Another mode is to pass through all the degrees, spending a year and a day in St. Michael's Square, being steeped in Cologne water, and perfumed, and dined, and introduced, and properly grounded in all the biography, and politics, and anecdotes of the boudoirs.

Yet these fineries may have grace and wit. Let there be grotesque sculpture about the gates and offices of temples. Let the creed and commandments even have the saucy hom-age of parody. The forms of politeness uni-versally express benevolence in superlative de-grees. What if they are in the mouths of selfish men, and used as means of selfishness? What

if the false gentleman almost bows the true out
of the world? What if the false gentleman contrives so to address his companion, as civilly
to exclude all others from his discourse, and
also to make them feel excluded? Real service will not lose its nobleness. All generosity
is not merely French and sentimental; nor is
it to be concealed, that living blood and a
passion of kindness does at last distinguish
God's gentleman from Fashion's. The epitaph
of Sir Jenkin Grout is not wholly unintelligible
to the present age. "Here lies Sir Jenkin
Grout, who loved his friend, and persuaded his
enemy: what his mouth ate, his hand paid for:
what his servants robbed, he restored: if a
woman gave him pleasure, he supported her in
pain: he never forgot his children: and whoso
touched his finger, drew after it his whole
body." Even the line of heroes is not utterly
extinct. There is still ever some admirable
person in plain clothes, standing on the wharf,
who jumps in to rescue a drowning man; there
is still some absurd inventor of charities; some
guide and comforter of runaway slaves; some
friend of Poland; some Philhellene; some
fanatic who plants shade-trees for the second

and third generation, and orchards when he is grown old; some well-concealed piety; some just man happy in an ill-fame; some youth ashamed of the favors of fortune, and impatiently casting them on other shoulders. And these are the centres of society, on which it returns for fresh impulses. These are the creators of Fashion, which is an attempt to organize beauty of behavior. The beautiful and the generous are, in the theory, the doctors and apostles of this church: Scipio, and the Cid, and Sir Philip Sidney, and Washington, and every pure and valiant heart, who worshipped Beauty by word and by deed. The persons who constitute the natural aristocracy, are not found in the actual aristocracy, or, only on its edge; as the chemical energy of the spectrum is found to be greatest just outside of the spectrum. Yet that is the infirmity of the seneschals, who do not know their sovereign, when he appears. The theory of society supposes the existence and sovereignty of these. It divines afar off their coming. It says with the elder gods,—

" As Heaven and Earth are fairer far
  Than Chaos and blank Darkness, though once chiefs;

And as we show beyond that Heaven and Earth,
In form and shape compact and beautiful ;
So, on our heels a fresh perfection treads ;
A power, more strong in beauty, born of us,
And fated to excel us, as we pass
In glory that old Darkness :
—————   for, 'tis the eternal law,
That first in beauty shall be first in might."

Therefore, within the ethnical circle of good society, there is a narrower and higher circle, concentration of its light, and flower of courtesy, to which there is always a tacit appeal of pride and reference, as to its inner and imperial court, the parliament of love and chivalry. And this is constituted of those persons in whom heroic dispositions are native, with the love of beauty, the delight in society, and the power to embellish the passing day. If the individuals who compose the purest circles of aristocracy in Europe, the guarded blood of centuries, should pass in review, in such manner as that we could, at leisure, and critically inspect their behavior, we might find no gentleman, and no lady ; for, although excellent specimens of courtesy and high-breeding would gratify us in the assemblage, in the particulars, we should detect offence. Because, elegance comes of no

36

breeding, but of birth.   There must be romance of character, or the most fastidious exclusion of impertinencies will not avail.   It must be genius which takes that direction : it must be not courteous, but courtesy.   High behavior is as rare in fiction, as it is in fact.   Scott is praised for the fidelity with which he painted the demeanor and conversation of the superior classes.   Certainly, kings and queens, nobles and great ladies, had some right to complain of the absurdity that had been put in their mouths, before the days of Waverley ; but nei- ther does Scott's dialogue bear criticism.   His lords brave each other in smart epigrammatic speeches, but the dialogue is in costume, and does not please on the second reading : it is not warm with life.   In Shakspeare alone, the speakers do not strut and bridle, the dialogue is easily great, and he adds to so many titles that of being the best-bred man in England, and in Christendom.   Once or twice in a life- time we are permitted to enjoy the charm of noble manners, in the presence of a man or woman who have no bar in their nature, but whose character emanates freely in their word and gesture.   A beautiful form is better than a beautiful face; a beautiful behavior is better than a beautiful form : it gives a higher pleasure than statues or pictures; it is the finest of the fine arts. A man is but a little thing in the midst of the objects of nature, yet, by the moral quality radiating from his countenance, he may abolish all considerations of magnitude, and in his manners equal the majesty of the world. I have seen an individual, whose manners, though wholly within the conventions of elegant society, were never learned there, but were original and commanding, and held out protection and prosperity; one who did not need the aid of a court-suit, but carried the holiday in his eye; who exhilarated the fancy by flinging wide the doors of new modes of existence; who shook off the captivity of etiquette, with happy, spirited bearing, good-natured and free as Robin Hood; yet with the port of an emperor,—if need be, calm, serious, and fit to stand the gaze of millions.

The open air and the fields, the street and public chambers, are the places where Man executes his will; let him yield or divide the sceptre at the door of the house. Woman, with her instinct of behavior, instantly detects in man a love of trifles, any coldness or imbecility, or, in short, any want of that large, flowing, and magnanimous deportment, which is indispensable as an exterior in the hall. Our American institutions have been friendly to her, and at this moment, I esteem it a chief felicity of this country, that it excels in women. A certain awkward consciousness of inferiority in the men, may give rise to the new chivalry in behalf of Woman's Rights. Certainly, let her be as much better placed in the laws and in social forms, as the most zealous reformer can ask, but I confide so entirely in her inspiring and musical nature, that I believe only herself can show us how she shall be served. The wonderful generosity of her sentiments raises her at times into heroical and godlike regions, and verifies the pictures of Minerva, Juno, or Polymnia; and, by the firmness with which she treads her upward path, she convinces the coarsest calculators that another road exists, than that which their feet know. But besides those who make good in our imagination the place of muses and of Delphic Sibyls, are there not women who fill our vase with wine and roses to the brim, so that the wine runs over

and fills the house with perfume; who inspire
us with courtesy; who unloose our tongues, and
we speak; who anoint our eyes, and we see?
We say things we never thought to have said;
for once, our walls of habitual reserve vanished,
and left us at large; we were children playing
with children in a wide field of flowers. Steep
us, we cried, in these influences, for days, for
weeks, and we shall be sunny poets, and will
write out in many-colored words the romance
that you are. Was it Hafiz or Firdousi that
said of his Persian Lilla, She was an elemental
force, and astonished me by her amount of life,
when I saw her day after day radiating, every
instant, redundant joy and grace on all around
her. She was a solvent powerful to reconcile
all heterogeneous persons into one society: like
air or water, an element of such a great range
of affinities, that it combines readily with a
thousand substances. Where she is present,
all others will be more than they are wont.
She was a unit and whole, so that whatsoever
she did, became her. She had too much sympathy and desire to please, than that you could
say, her manners were marked with dignity, yet
no princess could surpass her clear and erect

demeanor on each occasion. She did not study the Persian grammar, nor the books of the seven poets, but all the poems of the seven seemed to be written upon her. For, though the bias of her nature was not to thought, but to sympathy, yet was she so perfect in her own nature, as to meet intellectual persons by the fulness of her heart, warming them by her sentiments; believing, as she did, that by dealing nobly with all, all would show themselves noble.

I know that this Byzantine pile of chivalry or Fashion, which seems so fair and picturesque to those who look at the contemporary facts for science or for entertainment, is not equally pleasant to all spectators. The constitution of our society makes it a giant's castle to the ambitious youth who have not found their names enrolled in its Golden Book, and whom it has excluded from its coveted honors and privileges. They have yet to learn that its seeming grandeur is shadowy and relative: it is great by their allowance: its proudest gates will fly open at the approach of their courage and virtue. For the present distress, however, of those who are predisposed to suffer from the tyrannies of this caprice, there are easy remedies. To remove your residence a couple of miles, or at most four, will commonly relieve the most extreme susceptibility. For, the advantages which fashion values, are plants which thrive in very confined localities, in a few streets, namely. Out of this precinct, they go for nothing; are of no use in the farm, in the forest, in the market, in war, in the nuptial society, in the literary or scientific circle, at sea, in friendship, in the heaven of thought or virtue.

But we have lingered long enough in these painted courts. The worth of the thing signified must vindicate our taste for the emblem. Everything that is called fashion and courtesy humbles itself before the cause and fountain of honor, creator of titles and dignities, namely, the heart of love. This is the royal blood, this the fire, which, in all countries and contingencies, will work after its kind, and conquer and expand all that approaches it. This gives new meanings to every fact. This impoverishes the rich, suffering no grandeur but its own. What *is* rich? Are you rich enough to help anybody? to succor the unfashionable and the eccentric? rich enough to make the Canadian in his wagon, the itinerant with his consul's paper which commends him "To the charitable," the swarthy Italian with his few broken words of English, the lame pauper hunted by overseers from town to town, even the poor insane or besotted wreck of man or woman, feel the noble exception of your presence and your house, from the general bleakness and stoniness; to make such feel that they were greeted with a voice which made them both remember and hope? What is vulgar, but to refuse the claim on acute and conclusive reasons? What is gentle, but to allow it, and give their heart and yours one holiday from the national caution? Without the rich heart, wealth is an ugly beggar. The king of Schiraz could not afford to be so bountiful as the poor Osman who dwelt at his gate. Osman had a humanity so broad and deep, that although his speech was so bold and free with the Koran, as to disgust all the dervishes, yet was there never a poor outcast, eccentric, or insane man, some fool who had cut off his beard, or who had been mutilated under a vow, or had a pet madness in his brain, but fled at once to him,—that great heart lay there so sunny and hospitable in the centre of the country,—that it seemed as if the instinct of all sufferers drew them to his side. And the madness which he harbored, he did not share. Is not this to be rich? this only to be rightly rich?

But I shall hear without pain, that I play the courtier very ill, and talk of that which I do not well understand. It is easy to see, that what is called by distinction society and fashion, has good laws as well as bad, has much that is necessary, and much that is absurd. Too good for banning, and too bad for blessing, it reminds us of a tradition of the pagan mythology, in any attempt to settle its character. 'I overheard Jove, one day,' said Silenus, 'talking of destroying the earth; he said, it had failed; they were all rogues and vixens, who went from bad to worse, as fast as the days succeeded each other. Minerva said, she hoped not; they were only ridiculous little creatures, with this odd circumstance, that they had a blur, or indeterminate aspect, seen far or seen near; if you called them bad, they would appear so; if you called them good, they would appear so; and there was no one person or action among them, which would not puzzle her owl, much more all Olympus, to know whether it was fundamentally bad or good.'

GIFTS.

———

Gifts of one who loved me,—
'T was high time they came;
When he ceased to love me,
Time they stopped for shame.

(171)

ESSAY V.

GIFTS.

———

IT is said that the world is in a state of bank-ruptcy, that the world owes the world more than the world can pay, and ought to go into chancery, and be sold. I do not think this general insolvency, which involves in some sort all the population, to be the reason of the dif-ficulty experienced at Christmas and New Year, and other times, in bestowing gifts; since it is always so pleasant to be generous, though very vexatious to pay debts. But the impediment lies in the choosing. If, at any time, it comes into my head, that a present is due from me to somebody, I am puzzled what to give, until the opportunity is gone. Flowers and fruits are always fit presents; flowers, because they are a proud assertion that a ray of beauty outvalues all the utilities of the world. These gay natures contrast with the somewhat stern countenance of ordinary nature: they are like music heard

(173)

out of a work-house.   Nature does not cocker
us: we are children, not pets: she is not fond:
everything is dealt to us without fear or favor,
after severe universal laws.   Yet these delicate
flowers look like the frolic and interference of
love and beauty.   Men use to tell us that we
love flattery, even though we are not deceived
by it, because it shows that we are of importance enough to be courted.   Something like
that pleasure, the flowers give us: what am I
to whom these sweet hints are addressed?
Fruits are acceptable gifts, because they are the
flower of commodities, and admit of fantastic
values being attached to them.   If a man should
send to me to come a hundred miles to visit
him, and should set before me a basket of fine
summer-fruit, I should think there was some
proportion between the labor and the reward.

For common gifts, necessity makes pertinen-
ces and beauty every day, and one is glad when
an imperative leaves him no option, since if the
man at the door have no shoes, you have not
to consider whether you could procure him a
paint-box.   And as it is always pleasing to see
a man eat bread, or drink water, in the house
or out of doors, so it is always a great satisfaction

to supply these first wants.   Necessity does
everything well.   In our condition of universal
dependence, it seems heroic to let the petitioner
be the judge of his necessity, and to give all that
is asked, though at great inconvenience.   If it
be a fantastic desire, it is better to leave to
others the office of punishing him.   I can think
of many parts I should prefer playing to that of
the Furies.   Next to things of necessity, the
rule for a gift, which one of my friends pre-
scribed, is, that we might convey to some person
that which properly belonged to his character,
and was easily associated with him in thought.
But our tokens of compliment and love are for the
most part barbarous.   Rings and other jewels
are not gifts, but apologies for gifts.   The only
gift is a portion of thyself.   Thou must bleed
for me.   Therefore the poet brings his poem;
the shepherd, his lamb; the farmer, corn; the
miner, a gem; the sailor, coral and shells; the
painter, his picture; the girl, a handkerchief of
her own sewing.   This is right and pleasing,
for it restores society in so far to its primary
basis, when a man's biography is conveyed in
his gift, and every man's wealth is an index of
his merit.   But it is a cold, lifeless business

when you go to the shops to buy me something, which does not represent your life and talent, but a goldsmith's. This is fit for kings, and rich men who represent kings, and a false state of property, to make presents of gold and silver stuffs, as a kind of symbolical sin-offering, or payment of black-mail.

The law of benefits is a difficult channel, which requires careful sailing, or rude boats. It is not the office of a man to receive gifts. How dare you give them? We wish to be self-sustained. We do not quite forgive a giver. The hand that feeds us is in some danger of being bitten. We can receive anything from love, for that is a way of receiving it from ourselves; but not from any one who assumes to bestow. We sometimes hate the meat which we eat, because there seems something of degrading dependence in living by it.

> " Brother, if Jove to thee a present make,
>   Take heed that from his hands thou nothing take."

We ask the whole. Nothing less will content us. We arraign society, if it do not give us besides earth, and fire, and water, opportunity, love, reverence, and objects of veneration.

He is a good man, who can receive a gift well. We are either glad or sorry at a gift, and both emotions are unbecoming. Some violence, I think, is done, some degradation borne, when I rejoice or grieve at a gift. I am sorry when my independence is invaded, or when a gift comes from such as do not know my spirit, and so the act is not supported; and if the gift pleases me overmuch, then I should be ashamed that the donor should read my heart, and see that I love his commodity, and not him. The gift, to be true, must be the flowing of the giver unto me, correspondent to my flowing unto him. When the waters are at level, then my goods pass to him, and his to me. All his are mine, all mine his. I say to him, How can you give me this pot of oil, or this flagon of wine, when all your oil and wine is mine, which belief of mine this gift seems to deny? Hence the fitness of beautiful, not useful things for gifts. This giving is flat usurpation, and therefore when the beneficiary is ungrateful, as all beneficiaries hate all Timons, not at all considering the value of the gift, but looking back to the greater store it was taken from, I rather sympathize with the beneficiary, than with the anger

37

of my lord Timon. For, the expectation of gratitude is mean, and is continually punished by the total insensibility of the obliged person. It is a great happiness to get off without injury and heart-burning, from one who has had the ill luck to be served by you. It is a very onerous business, this of being served, and the debtor naturally wishes to give you a slap. A golden text for these gentlemen is that which I so admire in the Buddhist, who never thanks, and who says, "Do not flatter your benefactors."

The reason of these discords I conceive to be, that there is no commensurability between a man and any gift. You cannot give anything to a magnanimous person. After you have served him, he at once puts you in debt by his magnanimity. The service a man renders his friend is trivial and selfish, compared with the service he knows his friend stood in readiness to yield him, alike before he had begun to serve his friend, and now also. Compared with that good-will I bear my friend, the benefit it is in my power to render him seems small. Besides, our action on each other, good as well as evil, is so incidental and at random that we can seldom hear the acknowledgments of any person who would thank us for a benefit, without some shame and humiliation. We can rarely strike a direct stroke, but must be content with an oblique one; we seldom have the satisfaction of yielding a direct benefit, which is directly received. But rectitude scatters favors on every side without knowing it, and receives with wonder the thanks of all people.

I fear to breathe any treason against the majesty of love, which is the genius and god of gifts, and to whom we must not affect to prescribe. Let him give kingdoms or flower-leaves indifferently. There are persons, from whom we always expect fairy tokens; let us not cease to expect them. This is prerogative, and not to be limited by our municipal rules. For the rest, I like to see that we cannot be bought and sold. The best of hospitality and of generosity is also not in the will, but in fate. I find that I am not much to you; you do not need me; you do not feel me; then am I thrust out of doors, though you proffer me house and lands. No services are of any value, but only likeness. When I have attempted to join myself to others by services, it proved an intel-

lectual trick,—no more.   They eat your service
like apples, and leave you out.   But love them,
and they feel you, and delight in you all the
time.

NATURE.

The rounded world is fair to see,
Nine times folded in mystery:
Though baffled seers cannot impart
The secret of its laboring heart,
Throb thine with Nature's throbbing breast,
And all is clear from east to west.
Spirit that lurks each form within
Beckons to spirit of its kin;
Self-kindled every atom glows,
And hints the future which it owes.

(181)

ESSAY VI.

NATURE.

———

THERE are days which occur in this climate, at almost any season of the year, wherein the world reaches its perfection, when the air, the heavenly bodies, and the earth, make a harmony, as if nature would indulge her offspring; when, in these bleak upper sides of the planet, nothing is to desire that we have heard of the happiest latitudes, and we bask in the shining hours of Florida and Cuba; when everything that has life gives sign of satisfaction, and the cattle that lie on the ground seem to have great and tranquil thoughts. These halcyons may be looked for with a little more assurance in that pure October weather, which we distinguish by the name of the Indian Summer. The day, immeasurably long, sleeps over the broad hills and warm wide fields. To have lived through all its sunny hours, seems longevity enough. The solitary places do not seem quite lonely.

At the gates of the forest, the surprised man of the world is forced to leave his city estimates of great and small, wise and foolish. The knapsack of custom falls off his back with the first step he makes into these precincts. Here is sanctity which shames our religions, and reality which discredits our heroes. Here we find nature to be the circumstance which dwarfs every other circumstance, and judges like a god all men that come to her. We have crept out of our close and crowded houses into the night and morning, and we see what majestic beauties daily wrap us in their bosom. How willingly we would escape the barriers which render them comparatively impotent, escape the sophistication and second thought, and suffer nature to intrance us. The tempered light of the woods is like a perpetual morning, and is stimulating and heroic. The anciently reported spells of these places creep on us. The stems of pines, hemlocks, and oaks, almost gleam like iron on the excited eye. The incommunicable trees begin to persuade us to live with them, and quit our life of solemn trifles. Here no history, or church, or state, is interpolated on the divine sky and the immortal year. How easily we might walk onward into the opening landscape, absorbed by new pictures, and by thoughts fast succeeding each other, until by degrees the recollection of home was crowded out of the mind, all memory obliterated by the tyranny of the present, and we were led in triumph by nature.

These enchantments are medicinal, they sober and heal us. These are plain pleasures, kindly and native to us. We come to our own, and make friends with matter, which the ambitious chatter of the schools would persuade us to despise. We never can part with it; the mind loves its old home: as water to our thirst, so is the rock, the ground, to our eyes, and hands, and feet. It is firm water: it is cold flame: what health, what affinity! Ever an old friend, ever like a dear friend and brother, when we chat affectedly with strangers, comes in this honest face, and takes a grave liberty with us, and shames us out of our nonsense. Cities give not the human senses room enough. We go out daily and nightly to feed the eyes on the horizon, and require so much scope, just as we need water for our bath. There are all degrees of natural influence, from these quarantine

powers of nature, up to her dearest and gravest
ministrations to the imagination and the soul.
There is the bucket of cold water from the
spring, the wood-fire to which the chilled
traveller rushes for safety,—and there is the
sublime moral of autumn and of noon. We
nestle in nature, and draw our living as parasites
from her roots and grains, and we receive
glances from the heavenly bodies, which call
us to solitude, and foretell the remotest future.
The blue zenith is the point in which romance
and reality meet.   I think, if we should be rapt
away into all that we dream of heaven, and
should converse with Gabriel and Uriel, the
upper sky would be all that would remain of
our furniture.

It seems as if the day was not wholly profane, in which we have given heed to some
natural object.   The fall of snowflakes in a still
air, preserving to each crystal its perfect form;
the blowing of sleet over a wide sheet of water,
and over plains, the waving rye-field, the mimic
waving of acres of houstonia, whose innumerable florets whiten and ripple before the eye;
the reflections of trees and flowers in glassy
lakes; the musical steaming odorous south

wind, which converts all trees to windharps; the crackling and spurting of hemlock in the flames; or of pine logs, which yield glory to the walls and faces in the sittingroom,—these are the music and pictures of the most ancient religion. My house stands in low land, with limited outlook, and on the skirt of the village. But I go with my friend to the shore of our little river, and with one stroke of the paddle, I leave the village politics and personalities, yes, and the world of villages and personalities behind, and pass into a delicate realm of sunset and moonlight, too bright almost for spotted man to enter without noviciate and probation. We penetrate bodily this incredible beauty: we dip our hands in this painted element: our eyes are bathed in these lights and forms. A holiday, a villeggiatura, a royal revel, the proudest, most heart-rejoicing festival that valor and beauty, power and taste, ever decked and enjoyed, establishes itself on the instant. These sunset clouds, these delicately emerging stars, with their private and ineffable glances, signify it and proffer it. I am taught the poorness of our invention, the ugliness of towns and palaces. Art and luxury have early learned that they must work as enhancement and sequel to this original beauty. I am overinstructed for my return. Henceforth I shall be hard to please. I cannot go back to toys. I am grown expensive and sophisticated. I can no longer live without elegance: but a countryman shall be my master of revels. He who knows the most, he who knows what sweets and virtues are in the ground, the waters, the plants, the heavens, and how to come at these enchantments, is the rich and royal man. Only as far as the masters of the world have called in nature to their aid, can they reach the height of magnificence. This is the meaning of their hanging-gardens, villas, garden-houses, islands, parks, and preserves, to back their faulty personality with these strong accessories. I do not wonder that the landed interest should be invincible in the state with these dangerous auxiliaries. These bribe and invite; not kings, not palaces, not men, not women, but these tender and poetic stars, eloquent of secret promises. We heard what the rich man said, we knew of his villa, his grove, his wine, and his company, but the provocation and point of the invitation came out of these beguiling stars. In their soft glances, I see

what men strove to realize in some Versailles,
or Paphos, or Ctesiphon. Indeed, it is the
magical lights of the horizon, and the blue sky
for the background, which save all our works
of art, which were otherwise bawbles. When
the rich tax the poor with servility and obse-
quiousness, they should consider the effect of
men reputed to be the possessors of nature, on
imaginative minds. Ah! if the rich were rich as
the poor fancy riches! A boy hears a military
band play on the field at night, and he has
kings and queens, and famous chivalry palpably
before him. He hears the echoes of a horn in
a hill country, in the Notch Mountains, for example, which converts the mountains into an
Æolian harp, and this supernatural *tiralira* restores to him the Dorian mythology, Apollo,
Diana, and all divine hunters and huntresses.
Can a musical note be so lofty, so haughtily
beautiful! To the poor young poet, thus fabu-
lous is his picture of society; he is loyal; he
respects the rich; they are rich for the sake of
his imagination; how poor his fancy would be,
if they were not rich! That they have some
high-fenced grove, which they call a park; that
they live in larger and better-garnished saloons

than he has visited, and go in coaches, keeping only the society of the elegant, to watering-places, and to distant cities, are the ground-work from which he has delineated estates of romance, compared with which their actual possessions are shanties and paddocks. The muse herself betrays her son, and enhances the gifts of wealth and well-born beauty, by a radiation out of the air, and clouds, and forests that skirt the road,—a certain haughty favor, as if from patrician genii to patricians, a kind of aristocracy in nature, a prince of the power of the air.

The moral sensibility which makes Edens and Tempes so easily, may not be always found, but the material landscape is never far off. We can find these enchantments without visiting the Como Lake, or the Madeira Islands. We exaggerate the praises of local scenery. In every landscape, the point of astonishment is the meeting of the sky and the earth, and that is seen from the first hillock as well as from the top of the Alleghanies. The stars at night stoop down over the brownest, homeliest common, with all the spiritual magnificence which they shed on the Campagna, or on the marble deserts of Egypt. The uprolled clouds and the colors of morning and evening, will transfigure maples and alders. The difference between landscape and landscape is small, but there is great difference in the beholders. There is nothing so wonderful in any particular landscape, as the necessity of being beautiful under which every landscape lies. Nature cannot be surprised in undress. Beauty breaks in everywhere.

But it is very easy to outrun the sympathy of readers on this topic, which schoolmen called *natura naturata*, or nature passive. One can hardly speak directly of it without excess. It is as easy to broach in mixed companies what is called "the subject of religion." A susceptible person does not like to indulge his tastes in this kind, without the apology of some trivial necessity: he goes to see a wood-lot, or to look at the crops, or to fetch a plant or a mineral from a remote locality, or he carries a fowling piece, or a fishing-rod. I suppose this shame must have a good reason. A dilettantism in nature is barren and unworthy. The fop of fields is no better than his brother of Broadway. Men are naturally hunters and inquisitive of wood-craft, and I suppose that such a gazetteer as wood-cutters and Indians should furnish facts for, would take place in the most sumptuous drawingrooms of all the "Wreaths" and "Flora's chaplets" of the bookshops; yet ordinarily, whether we are too clumsy for so subtle a topic, or from whatever cause, as soon as men begin to write on nature, they fall into euphuism. Frivolity is a most unfit tribute to Pan, who ought to be represented in the mythology as the most continent of gods. I would not be frivolous before the admirable reserve and prudence of time, yet I cannot renounce the right of returning often to this old topic. The multitude of false churches accredits the true religion. Literature, poetry, science, are the homage of man to this unfathomed secret, concerning which no sane man can affect an indifference or incuriosity. Nature is loved by what is best in us. It is loved as the city of God, although, or rather because there is no citizen. The sunset is unlike anything that is underneath it: it wants men. And the beauty of nature must always seem unreal and mocking, until the landscape has human figures, that are as good as itself. If there were good men,

there would never be this rapture in nature. If
the king is in the palace, nobody looks at the
walls. It is when he is gone, and the house is
filled with grooms and gazers, that we turn
from the people, to find relief in the majestic
men that are suggested by the pictures and the
architecture. The critics who complain of the
sickly separation of the beauty of nature from
the thing to be done, must consider that our
hunting of the picturesque is inseparable from
our protest against false society. Man is fallen;
nature is erect, and serves as a differential
thermometer, detecting the presence or absence
of the divine sentiment in man. By fault of
our dulness and selfishness, we are looking up
to nature, but when we are convalescent, nature
will look up to us. We see the foaming brook
with compunction: if our own life flowed with
the right energy, we should shame the brook.
The stream of zeal sparkles with real fire, and
not with reflex rays of sun and moon. Nature
may be as selfishly studied as trade. Astronomy to the selfish becomes astrology; psy-
chology, mesmerism (with intent to show
where our spoons are gone); and anatomy and
physiology, become phrenology and palmistry.

38

But taking timely warning, and leaving many
things unsaid on this topic, let us not longer
omit our homage to the Efficient Nature, *natura naturans*, the quick cause, before which all
forms flee as the driven snows, itself secret, its
works driven before it in flocks and multitudes,
(as the ancient represented nature by Proteus,
a shepherd,) and in undescribable variety. It
publishes itself in creatures, reaching from par-
ticles and spicula, through transformation on
transformation to the highest symmetries, arriv-
ing at consummate results without a shock or a
leap. A little heat, that is, a little motion, is
all that differences the bald, dazzling white, and
deadly cold poles of the earth from the prolific
tropical climates. All changes pass without
violence, by reason of the two cardinal conditions
of boundless space and boundless time. Geol-
ogy has initiated us into the secularity of nature, and taught us to disuse our dame-school
measures, and exchange our Mosaic and Ptole-
maic schemes for her large style. We knew
nothing rightly, for want of perspective. Now
we learn what patient periods must round themselves before the rock is formed, then before
the rock is broken, and the first lichen race has

disintegrated the thinnest external plate into soil, and opened the door for the remote Flora, Fauna, Ceres, and Pomona, to come in. How far off yet is the trilobite! how far the quadruped! how inconceivably remote is man! All duly arrive, and then race after race of men. It is a long way from granite to the oyster; farther yet to Plato, and the preaching of the immortality of the soul. Yet all must come, as surely as the first atom has two sides.

Motion or change, and identity or rest, are the first and second secrets of nature: Motion and Rest. The whole code of her laws may be written on the thumbnail, or the signet of a ring. The whirling bubble on the surface of a brook, admits us to the secret of the mechanics of the sky. Every shell on the beach is a key to it. A little water made to rotate in a cup explains the formation of the simpler shells; the addition of matter from year to year, arrives at last at the most complex forms; and yet so poor is nature with all her craft, that, from the beginning to the end of the universe, she has but one stuff,—but one stuff with its two ends, to serve up all her dream-like variety. Compound it how she will, star, sand, fire, water, tree, man, it is still one stuff, and betrays the same properties.

Nature is always consistent, though she feigns to contravene her own laws. She keeps her laws, and seems to transcend them. She arms and equips an animal to find its place and living in the earth, and, at the same time, she arms and equips another animal to destroy it. Space exists to divide creatures; but by clothing the sides of a bird with a few feathers, she gives him a petty omnipresence. The direction is forever onward, but the artist still goes back for materials, and begins again with the first elements on the most advanced stage: otherwise, all goes to ruin. If we look at her work, we seem to catch a glance of a system in transition. Plants are the young of the world, vessels of health and vigor; but they grope ever upward towards consciousness; the trees are imperfect men, and seem to bemoan their imprisonment, rooted in the ground. The animal is the novice and probationer of a more advanced order. The men, though young, having tasted the first drop from the cup of thought, are already dissipated: the maples and ferns are still uncorrupt; yet no doubt, when they

come to consciousness, they too will curse and
swear. Flowers so strictly belong to youth,
that we adult men soon come to feel, that their
beautiful generations concern not us: we have
had our day; now let the children have theirs.
The flowers jilt us, and we are old bachelors
with our ridiculous tenderness.

Things are so strictly related, that according
to the skill of the eye, from any one object the
parts and properties of any other may be pre-
dicted. If we had eyes to see it, a bit of stone
from the city wall would certify us of the
necessity that man must exist, as readily as the
city. That identity makes us all one, and reduces to nothing great intervals on our custom-
ary scale. We talk of deviations from natural
life, as if artificial life were not also natural. The
smoothest curled courtier in the boudoirs of a
palace has an animal nature, rude and aboriginal
as a white bear, omnipotent to its own ends,
and is directly related, there amid essences and
billetsdoux, to Himmaleh mountain-chains, and
the axis of the globe. If we consider how much
we are nature's, we need not be superstitious
about towns, as if that terrific or benefic force
did not find us there also, and fashion cities.

Nature who made the mason, made the house. We may easily hear too much of rural influences. The cool disengaged air of natural objects, makes them enviable to us, chafed and irritable creatures with red faces, and we think we shall be as grand as they, if we camp out and eat roots; but let us be men instead of wood-chucks, and the oak and the elm shall gladly serve us, though we sit in chairs of ivory on carpets of silk.

This guiding identity runs through all the surprises and contrasts of the piece, and characterizes every law. Man carries the world in his head, the whole astronomy and chemistry suspended in a thought. Because the history of nature is charactered in his brain, therefore is he the prophet and discoverer of her secrets. Every known fact in natural science was divined by the presentiment of somebody, before it was actually verified. A man does not tie his shoe without recognising laws which bind the farthest regions of nature : moon, plant, gas, crystal, are concrete geometry and numbers. Common sense knows its own, and recognises the fact at first sight in chemical experiment. The common sense of Franklin, Dalton, Davy, and Black, is the same common sense which made the arrangements which now it discovers.

If the identity expresses organized rest, the counter action runs also into organization. The astronomers said, ' Give us matter, and a little motion, and we will construct the universe. It is not enough that we should have matter, we must also have a single impulse, one shove to launch the mass, and generate the harmony of the centrifugal and centripetal forces. Once heave the ball from the hand, and we can show how all this mighty order grew.'—' A very unreasonable postulate,' said the metaphysicians, ' and a plain begging of the question. Could you not prevail to know the genesis of projection, as well as the continuation of it?' Nature, meanwhile, had not waited for the discussion, but, right or wrong, bestowed the impulse, and the balls rolled. It was no great affair, a mere push, but the astronomers were right in making much of it, for there is no end to the consequences of the act. That famous aboriginal push propagates itself through all the balls of the system, and through every atom of every ball, through all the races of crea- tures, and through the history and performances of every individual. Exaggeration is in the course of things. Nature sends no creature, no man into the world, without adding a small excess of his proper quality. Given the planet, it is still necessary to add the impulse; so, to every creature nature added a little violence of direction in its proper path, a shove to put it on its way; in every instance, a slight generosity, a drop too much. Without electricity the air would rot, and without this violence of direction, which men and women have, without a spice of bigot and fanatic, no excitement, no efficiency. We aim above the mark, to hit the mark. Every act hath some falsehood of exaggeration in it. And when now and then comes along some sad, sharp-eyed man, who sees how paltry a game is played, and refuses to play, but blabs the secret;—how then? is the bird flown? O no, the wary Nature sends a new troop of fairer forms, of lordlier youths, with a little more excess of direction to hold them fast to their several aim; makes them a little wrongheaded in that direction in which they are rightest, and on goes the game again with new whirl, for a generation or two more. The child with his sweet pranks, the fool of his senses, commanded by every sight and sound, without any power to compare and rank his sensations, abandoned to a whistle or a painted chip, to a lead dragoon, or a gingerbread-dog, individualizing everything, generalizing nothing, delighted with every new thing, lies down at night overpowered by the fatigue, which this day of continual pretty madness has incurred. But Nature has answered her purpose with the curly, dimpled lunatic. She has tasked every faculty, and has secured the symmetrical growth of the bodily frame, by all these attitudes and exertions,—an end of the first importance, which could not be trusted to any care less perfect than her own. This glitter, this opaline lustre plays round the top of every toy to his eye, to ensure his fidelity, and he is deceived to his good. We are made alive and kept alive by the same arts. Let the stoics say what they please, we do not eat for the good of living, but because the meat is savory and the appetite is keen. The vegetable life does not content itself with casting from the flower or the tree a single seed, but it fills the air and earth with a pro- digality of seeds, that, if thousands perish, thousands may plant themselves, that hundreds may come up, that tens may live to maturity, that, at least, one may replace the parent. All things betray the same calculated profusion. The excess of fear with which the animal frame is hedged round, shrinking from cold, starting at sight of a snake, or at a sudden noise, protects us, through a multitude of groundless alarms, from some one real danger at last. The lover seeks in marriage his private felicity and perfection, with no prospective end; and nature hides in his happiness her own end, namely, progeny, or the perpetuity of the race.

But the craft with which the world is made, runs also into the mind and character of men. No man is quite sane; each has a vein of folly in his composition, a slight determination of blood to the head, to make sure of holding him hard to some one point which nature had taken to heart. Great causes are never tried on their merits; but the cause is reduced to particulars to suit the size of the partizans, and the contention is ever hottest on minor matters. Not less remarkable is the overfaith of each man in the importance of what he has to do or say. The poet, the prophet, has a higher value for what he utters than any hearer, and therefore it gets spoken. The strong, self-complacent Luther declares with an emphasis, not to be mistaken, that "God himself cannot do without wise men." Jacob Behmen and George Fox betray their egotism in the pertinacity of their controversial tracts, and James Naylor once suffered himself to be worshipped as the Christ. Each prophet comes presently to identify himself with his thought, and to esteem his hat and shoes sacred. However this may discredit such persons with the judicious, it helps them with the people, as it gives heat, pungency, and publicity to their words. A similar experience is not infrequent in private life. Each young and ardent person writes a diary, in which, when the hours of prayer and penitence arrive, he inscribes his soul. The pages thus written are, to him, burning and fragrant: he reads them on his knees by midnight and by the morning star; he wets them with his tears: they are sacred; too good for the world, and hardly yet to be shown to the dearest friend. This is the man-child that is born to the soul, and her life still circulates in the babe. The umbilical cord has not yet been cut. After some time has elapsed, he begins to wish to admit his friend to this hallowed experience, and with hesitation, yet with firmness, exposes the pages to his eye. Will they not burn his eyes? The friend coldly turns them over, and passes from the writing to conversation, with easy transition, which strikes the other party with astonishment and vexation. He cannot suspect the writing itself. Days and nights of fervid life, of communion with angels of darkness and of light, have engraved their shadowy characters on that tear-stained book. He suspects the intelligence or the heart of his friend. Is there then no friend? He cannot yet credit that one may have impressive experience, and yet may not know how to put his private fact into literature; and perhaps the discovery that wisdom has other tongues and ministers than we, that though we should hold our peace, the truth would not the less be spoken, might check injuriously the flames of our zeal. A man can only speak, so long as he does not feel his speech to be partial and inadequate. It is partial, but he does not see it to be so, whilst he utters it. As soon as he is released from the instinctive and particular, and sees its partiality, he shuts his mouth in disgust. For, no man

can write anything, who does not think that
what he writes is for the time the history of the
world; or do anything well, who does not
esteem his work to be of importance. My work
may be of none, but I must not think it of none,
or I shall not do it with impunity.

In like manner, there is throughout nature
something mocking, something that leads us on
and on, but arrives nowhere, keeps no faith with
us. All promise outruns the performance.
We live in a system of approximations. Every
end is prospective of some other end, which is
also temporary; a round and final success nowhere. We are encamped in nature, not domesticated. Hunger and thirst lead us on to
eat and to drink; but bread and wine, mix and
cook them how you will, leave us hungry and
thirsty, after the stomach is full. It is the
same with all our arts and performances. Our
music, our poetry, our language itself are not
satisfactions, but suggestions. The hunger for
wealth, which reduces the planet to a garden,
fools the eager pursuer. What is the end
sought? Plainly to secure the ends of good
sense and beauty, from the intrusion of defor-
mity or vulgarity of any kind. But what an

operose method! What a train of means to secure a little conversation! This palace of brick and stone, these servants, this kitchen, these stables, horses and equipage, this bank-stock, and file of mortgages; trade to all the world, country-house and cottage by the water-side, all for a little conversation, high, clear, and spiritual! Could it not be had as well by beggars on the highway? No, all these things came from successive efforts of these beggars to remove friction from the wheels of life, and give opportunity. Conversation, character, were the avowed ends; wealth was good as it appeased the animal cravings, cured the smoky chimney, silenced the creaking door, brought friends together in a warm and quiet room, and kept the children and the dinner-table in a different apartment. Thought, virtue, beauty, were the ends; but it was known that men of thought and virtue sometimes had the headache, or wet feet, or could lose good time whilst the room was getting warm in winter days. Unluckily, in the exertions necessary to remove these inconveniences, the main attention has been diverted to this object; the old aims have been lost sight of, and to remove friction has come to be the end. That is the ridicule of rich men, and Boston, London, Vienna, and now the governments generally of the world, are cities and governments of the rich, and the masses are not men, but *poor men*, that is, men who would be rich; this is the ridicule of the class, that they arrive with pains and sweat and fury nowhere; when all is done, it is for nothing. They are like one who has interrupted the conversation of a company to make his speech, and now has forgotten what he went to say. The appearance strikes the eye everywhere of an aimless society, of aimless nations. Were the ends of nature so great and cogent, as to exact this immense sacrifice of men?

Quite analogous to the deceits in life, there is, as might be expected, a similar effect on the eye from the face of external nature. There is in woods and waters a certain enticement and flattery, together with a failure to yield a present satisfaction. This disappointment is felt in every landscape. I have seen the softness and beauty of the summer-clouds floating feathery overhead, enjoying, as it seemed, their height and privilege of motion, whilst yet they appeared not so much the drapery of this place and hour, as forelooking to some pavilions and gardens of festivity beyond. It is an odd jealousy: but the poet finds himself not near enough to his object. The pine-tree, the river, the bank of flowers before him, does not seem to be nature. Nature is still elsewhere. This or this is but outskirt and far-off reflection and echo of the triumph that has passed by, and is now at its glancing splendor and heyday, perchance in the neighboring fields, or, if you stand in the field, then in the adjacent woods. The present object shall give you this sense of stillness that follows a pageant which has just gone by. What splendid distance, what recesses of ineffable pomp and loveliness in the sunset! But who can go where they are, or lay his hand or plant his foot thereon? Off they fall from the round world forever and ever. It is the same among the men and women, as among the silent trees; always a referred existence, an absence, never a presence and satisfaction. Is it, that beauty can never be grasped? in persons and in landscape is equally inaccessible? The accepted and betrothed lover has lost the wildest charm of his maiden in her acceptance of him. She was heaven whilst he pursued her as a star : she cannot be heaven, if she stoops to such a one as he.

What shall we say of this omnipresent appearance of that first projectile impulse, of this flattery and baulking of so many well-meaning creatures ? Must we not suppose somewhere in the universe a slight treachery and derision ? Are we not engaged to a serious resentment of this use that is made of us? Are we tickled trout, and fools of nature ? One look at the face of heaven and earth lays all petulance at rest, and soothes us to wiser convictions. To the intelligent, nature converts itself into a vast promise, and will not be rashly explained. Her secret is untold. Many and many an Œdipus arrives : he has the whole mystery teeming in his brain. Alas ! the same sorcery has spoiled his skill ; no syllable can he shape on his lips. Her mighty orbit vaults like the fresh rainbow into the deep, but no archangel's wing was yet strong enough to follow it, and report of the return of the curve. But it also appears, that our actions are seconded and disposed to greater conclusions than we designed. We are escorted on every hand through life by spiritual agents, and a beneficent purpose lies in wait for us.

39

We cannot bandy words with nature, or deal with her as we deal with persons. If we measure our individual forces against hers, we may easily feel as if we were the sport of an insuperable destiny. But if, instead of identifying ourselves with the work, we feel that the soul of the workman streams through us, we shall find the peace of the morning dwelling first in our hearts, and the fathomless powers of gravity and chemistry and, over them, of life, pre-existing within us in their highest form.

The uneasiness which the thought of our helplessness in the chain of causes occasions us, results from looking too much at one condition of nature, namely, Motion. But the drag is never taken from the wheel. Wherever the impulse exceeds, the Rest or Identity insinuates its compensation. All over the wide fields of earth grows the prunella or self-heal. After every foolish day we sleep off the fumes and furies of its hours; and though we are always engaged with particulars, and often enslaved to them, we bring with us to every experiment the innate universal laws. These, while they exist in the mind as ideas, stand around us in nature forever embodied, a present sanity to expose

and cure the insanity of men. Our servitude
to particulars betrays into a hundred foolish ex-
pectations. We anticipate a new era from the
invention of a locomotive, or a balloon; the
new engine brings with it the old checks.
They say that by electro-magnetism, your salad
shall be grown from the seed, whilst your fowl
is roasting for dinner: it is a symbol of our
modern aims and endeavors,—of our condensa-
tion and acceleration of objects: but nothing is
gained: nature cannot be cheated: man's life is
but seventy salads long, grow they swift or
grow they slow. In these checks and impossi-
bilities, however, we find our advantage, not less
than in the impulses. Let the victory fall
where it will, we are on that side. And the
knowledge that we traverse the whole scale of
being, from the centre to the poles of nature,
and have some stake in every possibility, lends
that sublime lustre to death, which philosophy
and religion have too outwardly and literally
striven to express in the popular doctrine of
the immortality of the soul. The reality is
more excellent than the report. Here is no
ruin, no discontinuity, no spent ball. The
divine circulations never rest nor linger. Nature

is the incarnation of a thought, and turns to a thought again, as ice becomes water and gas. The world is mind precipitated, and the volatile essence is forever escaping again into the state of free thought. Hence the virtue and pungency of the influence on the mind, of natural objects, whether inorganic or organized. Man imprisoned, man crystallized, man vegetative, speaks to man impersonated. That power which does not respect quantity, which makes the whole and the particle its equal channel, delegates its smile to the morning, and distils its essence into every drop of rain. Every moment instructs, and every object: for wisdom is infused into every form. It has been poured into us as blood; it convulsed us as pain; it slid into us as pleasure; it enveloped us in dull, melancholy days, or in days of cheerful labor; we did not guess its essence, until after a long time.

POLITICS.

Gold and iron are good
To buy iron and gold;
All earth's fleece and food
For their like are sold.
Boded Merlin wise,
Proved Napoleon great,—
Nor kind nor coinage buys
Aught above its rate.
Fear, Craft, and Avarice
Cannot rear a State.
Out of dust to build
What is more than dust,—
Walls Amphion piled
Phœbus stablish must.
When the Muses nine
With the Virtues meet,
Find to their design
An Atlantic seat,
By green orchard boughs
Fended from the heat,
Where the statesman ploughs
Furrow for the wheat;
When the Church is social worth,
When the state-house is the hearth,
Then the perfect State is come,
The republican at home.

(213)

ESSAY VII.

POLITICS.

In dealing with the State, we ought to remember that its institutions are not aboriginal,
though they existed before we were born: that
they are not superior to the citizen: that every
one of them was once the act of a single man:
every law and usage was a man's expedient to
meet a particular case: that they all are imi-
table, all alterable; we may make as good; we
may make better. Society is an illusion to the
young citizen. It lies before him in rigid repose, with certain names, men, and institutions,
rooted like oak-trees to the centre, round which
all arrange themselves the best they can. But
the old statesman knows that society is fluid;
there are no such roots and centres; but any
particle may suddenly become the centre of the
movement, and compel the system to gyrate
round it, as every man of strong will, like
Pisistratus, or Cromwell, does for a time, and

every man of truth, like Plato, or Paul, does
forever. But politics rest on necessary foundations, and cannot be treated with levity. Re-
publics abound in young civilians, who believe
that the laws make the city, that grave modifications of the policy and modes of living, and
employments of the population, that commerce,
education, and religion, may be voted in or out;
and that any measure, though it were absurd,
may be imposed on a people, if only you can
get sufficient voices to make it a law. But the
wise know that foolish legislation is a rope of
sand, which perishes in the twisting; that the
State must follow, and not lead the character
and progress of the citizen; the strongest usurper
is quickly got rid of; and they only who build
on Ideas, build for eternity; and that the form
of government which prevails, is the expression
of what cultivation exists in the population
which permits it. The law is only a memo-
randum. We are superstitious, and esteem the
statute somewhat : so much life as it has in the
character of living men, is its force. The statute
stands there to say, yesterday we agreed so and
so, but how feel ye this article today? Our
statute is a currency, which we stamp with our

own portrait: it soon becomes unrecognizable, and in process of time will return to the mint. Nature is not democratic, nor limited-monarchical, but despotic, and will not be fooled or abated of any jot of her authority, by the pertest of her sons: and as fast as the public mind is opened to more intelligence, the code is seen to be brute and stammering. It speaks not articulately, and must be made to. Meantime the education of the general mind never stops. The reveries of the true and simple are prophetic. What the tender poetic youth dreams, and prays, and paints today, but shuns the ridicule of saying aloud, shall presently be the resolutions of public bodies, then shall be carried as grievance and bill of rights through conflict and war, and then shall be triumphant law and establishment for a hundred years, until it gives place, in turn, to new prayers and pictures. The history of the State sketches in coarse outline the progress of thought, and follows at a distance the delicacy of culture and of aspiration.

The theory of politics, which has possessed the mind of men, and which they have expressed the best they could in their laws and in

their revolutions, considers persons and property as the two objects for whose protection
government exists.   Of persons, all have equal
rights, in virtue of being identical in nature.
This interest, of course, with its whole power
demands a democracy.   Whilst the rights of
all as persons are equal, in virtue of their access
to reason, their rights in property are very unequal.   One man owns his clothes, and another
owns a county.   This accident, depending, primarily, on the skill and virtue of the parties, of
which there is every degree, and, secondarily,
on patrimony, falls unequally, and its rights,
of course, are unequal.   Personal rights, universally the same, demand a government framed
on the ratio of the census : property demands a
government framed on the ratio of owners and
of owning.   Laban, who has flocks and herds,
wishes them looked after by an officer on the
frontiers, lest the Midianites shall drive them
off, and pays a tax to that end.   Jacob has no
flocks or herds, and no fear of the Midianites,
and pays no tax to the officer.   It seemed fit
that Laban and Jacob should have equal rights
to elect the officer, who is to defend their persons, but that Laban, and not Jacob, should

elect the officer who is to guard the sheep and cattle. And, if question arise whether additional officers or watch-towers should be provided, must not Laban and Isaac, and those who must sell part of their herds to buy protection for the rest, judge better of this, and with more right, than Jacob, who, because he is a youth and a traveller, eats their bread and not his own.

In the earliest society the proprietors made their own wealth, and so long as it comes to the owners in the direct way, no other opinion would arise in any equitable community, than that property should make the law for property, and persons the law for persons.

But property passes through donation or inheritance to those who do not create it. Gift, in one case, makes it as really the new owner's, as labor made it the first owner's : in the other case, of patrimony, the law makes an ownership, which will be valid in each man's view according to the estimate which he sets on the public tranquillity.

It was not, however, found easy to embody the readily admitted principle, that property should make law for property, and persons for persons: since persons and property mixed themselves in every transaction. At last it seemed settled, that the rightful distinction was, that the proprietors should have more elective franchise than non-proprietors, on the Spartan principle of " calling that which is just, equal; not that which is equal, just."

That principle no longer looks so self-evident as it appeared in former times, partly, because doubts have arisen whether too much weight had not been allowed in the laws, to property, and such a structure given to our usages, as allowed the rich to encroach on the poor, and to keep them poor; but mainly, because there is an instinctive sense, however obscure and yet inarticulate, that the whole constitution of property, on its present tenures, is injurious, and its influence on persons deteriorating and degrading; that truly, the only interest for the consideration of the State, is persons: that property will always follow persons; that the highest end of government is the culture of men: and if men can be educated, the institutions will share their improvement, and the moral sentiment will write the law of the land.

If it be not easy to settle the equity of this

question, the peril is less when we take note of
our natural defences. We are kept by better
guards than the vigilance of such magistrates as
we commonly elect. Society always consists, in
greatest part, of young and foolish persons. The
old, who have seen through the hypocrisy of
courts and statesmen, die, and leave no wisdom
to their sons. They believe their own newspaper, as their fathers did at their age. With
such an ignorant and deceivable majority,
States would soon run to ruin, but that there
are limitations, beyond which the folly and
ambition of governors cannot go. Things have
their laws, as well as men; and things refuse to
be trifled with. Property will be protected.
Corn will not grow, unless it is planted and
manured; but the farmer will not plant or hoe
it, unless the chances are a hundred to one,
that he will cut and harvest it. Under any
forms, persons and property must and will have
their just sway. They exert their power, as
steadily as matter its attraction. Cover up a
pound of earth never so cunningly, divide and
subdivide it; melt it to liquid, convert it to gas;
it will always weigh a pound: it will always
attract and resist other matter, by the full virtue

of one pound weight;—and the attributes of a person, his wit and his moral energy, will exercise, under any law or extinguishing tyranny, their proper force,—if not overtly, then covertly; if not for the law, then against it; with right, or by might.

The boundaries of personal influence it is impossible to fix, as persons are organs of moral or supernatural force. Under the dominion of an idea, which possesses the minds of multitudes, as civil freedom, or the religious sentiment, the powers of persons are no longer subjects of calculation. A nation of men unanimously bent on freedom, or conquest, can easily confound the arithmetic of statists, and achieve extravagant actions, out of all proportion to their means; as, the Greeks, the Saracens, the Swiss, the Americans, and the French have done.

In like manner, to every particle of property belongs its own attraction. A cent is the representative of a certain quantity of corn or other commodity. Its value is in the necessities of the animal man. It is so much warmth, so much bread, so much water, so much land. The law may do what it will with the owner of property, its just power will still attach to the cent. The law may in a mad freak say, that all shall have power except the owners of property: they shall have no vote. Nevertheless, by a higher law, the property will, year after year, write every statute that respects property. The non-proprietor will be the scribe of the proprietor. What the owners wish to do, the whole power of property will do, either through the law, or else in defiance of it. Of course, I speak of all the property, not merely of the great estates. When the rich are outvoted, as frequently happens, it is the joint treasury of the poor which exceeds their accumulations. Every man owns something, if it is only a cow, or a wheelbarrow, or his arms, and so has that property to dispose of.

The same necessity which secures the rights of person and property against the malignity or folly of the magistrate, determines the form and methods of governing, which are proper to each nation, and to its habit of thought, and nowise transferable to other states of society. In this country, we are very vain of our political institutions, which are singular in this, that they sprung, within the memory of living men, from the character and condition of the people, which they still express with sufficient fidelity, —and we ostentatiously prefer them to any other in history. They are not better, but only fitter for us. We may be wise in asserting the advantage in modern times of the democratic form, but to other states of society, in which religion consecrated the monarchical, that and not this was expedient. Democracy is better for us, because the religious sentiment of the present time accords better with it. Born democrats, we are nowise qualified to judge of monarchy, which, to our fathers living in the monarchical idea, was also relatively right. But our institutions, though in coincidence with the spirit of the age, have not any exemption from the practical defects which have discredited other forms. Every actual State is corrupt. Good men must not obey the laws too well. What satire on government can equal the severity of censure conveyed in the word *politic*, which now for ages has signified *cunning*, intimating that the State is a trick?

The same benign necessity and the same practical abuse appear in the parties into which each State divides itself, of opponents and defenders of the administration of the government.

Parties are also founded on instincts, and have better guides to their own humble aims than the sagacity of their leaders. They have nothing perverse in their origin, but rudely mark some real and lasting relation. We might as wisely reprove the east wind, or the frost, as a political party, whose members, for the most part, could give no account of their position, but stand for the defence of those interests in which they find themselves. Our quarrel with them begins, when they quit this deep natural ground at the bidding of some leader, and, obeying personal considerations, throw themselves into the maintenance and defence of points, nowise belonging to their system. A party is perpetually corrupted by personality. Whilst we absolve the association from dishonesty we cannot extend the same charity to their leaders. They reap the rewards of the docility and zeal of the masses which they direct. Ordinarily, our parties are parties of circumstance, and not of principle; as, the planting interest in conflict with the commercial; the party of capitalists, and that of operatives; parties which are identical in their moral character, and which can easily change ground

40

with each other, in the support of many of their measures.   Parties of principle, as, religious sects, or the party of free-trade, of universal suffrage, of abolition of slavery, of abolition of capital punishment, degenerate into personalities, or would inspire enthusiasm.   The vice of our leading parties in this country (which may be cited as a fair specimen of these societies of opinion) is, that they do not plant themselves on the deep and necessary grounds to which they are respectively entitled, but lash themselves to fury in the carrying of some local and momentary measure, nowise useful to the commonwealth.   Of the two great parties, which, at this hour, almost share the nation between them, I should say, that, one has the best cause, and the other contains the best men.   The philosopher, the poet, or the religious man, will, of course, wish to cast his vote with the democrat, for free-trade, for wide suffrage, for the abolition of legal cruelties in the penal code, and for facilitating in every manner the access of the young and the poor to the sources of wealth and power.   But he can rarely accept the persons whom the so-called popular party propose to him as representatives of these liber-

alities. They have not at heart the ends which
give to the name of democracy what hope and
virtue are in it. The spirit of our American
radicalism is destructive and aimless: it is not
loving; it has no ulterior and divine ends; but
is destructive only out of hatred and selfishness.
On the other side, the conservative party, composed of the most moderate, able, and cultivated part of the population, is timid, and
merely defensive of property. It vindicates no
right, it aspires to no real good, it brands no
crime, it proposes no generous policy, it does
not build, nor write, nor cherish the arts, nor
foster religion, nor establish schools, nor en-
courage science, nor emancipate the slave, nor
befriend the poor, or the Indian, or the im-
migrant. From neither party, when in power,
has the world any benefit to expect in science,
art, or humanity, at all commensurate with the
resources of the nation.

I do not for these defects despair of our republic. We are not at the mercy of any waves
of chance. In the strife of ferocious parties,
human nature always finds itself cherished, as
the children of the convicts at Botany Bay are
found to have as healthy a moral sentiment as

other children.   Citizens of feudal states are
alarmed at our democratic institutions lapsing
into anarchy; and the older and more cautious
among ourselves are learning from Europeans
to look with some terror at our turbulent freedom.   It is said that in our license of constru-
ing the Constitution, and in the despotism of
public opinion, we have no anchor; and one
foreign observer thinks he has found the safe-
guard in the sanctity of Marriage among us;
and another thinks he has found it in our Calvinism.   Fisher Ames expressed the popular
security more wisely, when he compared a
monarchy and a republic, saying, "that a monarchy is a merchantman, which sails well, but
will sometimes strike on a rock, and go to the
bottom; whilst a republic is a raft, which would
never sink, but then your feet are always in
water."   No forms can have any dangerous
importance, whilst we are befriended by the
laws of things.   It makes no difference how
many tons weight of atmosphere presses on our
heads, so long as the same pressure resists it
within the lungs.   Augment the mass a thousand fold, it cannot begin to crush us, as long
as reaction is equal to action.   The fact of two

poles, of two forces, centripetal and centrifugal, is universal, and each force by its own activity develops the other. Wild liberty develops iron conscience. Want of liberty, by strengthening law and decorum, stupefies conscience. 'Lynch-law' prevails only where there is greater hardihood and self-subsistency in the leaders. A mob cannot be a permanency: everybody's interest requires that it should not exist, and only justice satisfies all.

We must trust infinitely to the beneficent necessity which shines through all laws. Human nature expresses itself in them as characteristically as in statues, or songs, or railroads, and an abstract of the codes of nations would be a transcript of the common conscience. Governments have their origin in the moral identity of men. Reason for one is seen to be reason for another, and for every other. There is a middle measure which satisfies all parties, be they never so many, or so resolute for their own. Every man finds a sanction for his simplest claims and deeds in decisions of his own mind, which he calls Truth and Holiness. In these decisions all the citizens find a perfect agreement, and only in these; not in what is good to eat, good to wear, good use of time, or what amount of land, or of public aid, each is entitled to claim. This truth and justice men presently endeavor to make application of, to the measuring of land, the apportionment of service, the protection of life and property. Their first endeavors, no doubt, are very awkward. Yet absolute right is the first governor; or, every government is an impure theocracy. The idea, after which each community is aiming to make and mend its law, is, the will of the wise man. The wise man, it cannot find in nature, and it makes awkward but earnest efforts to secure his government by contrivance; as, by causing the entire people to give their voices on every measure; or, by a double choice to get the representation of the whole; or, by a selection of the best citizens; or, to secure the advantages of efficiency and internal peace, by confiding the government to one, who may himself select his agents. All forms of government symbolize an immortal government, common to all dynasties and independent of numbers, perfect where two men exist, perfect where there is only one man.

Every man's nature is a sufficient advertisement to him of the character of his fellows.

My right and my wrong, is their right and their wrong. Whilst I do what is fit for me, and abstain from what is unfit, my neighbor and I shall often agree in our means, and work together for a time to one end. But whenever I find my dominion over myself not sufficient for me, and undertake the direction of him also, I overstep the truth, and come into false relations to him. I may have so much more skill or strength than he, that he cannot express adequately his sense of wrong, but it is a lie, and hurts like a lie both him and me. Love and nature cannot maintain the assumption: it must be executed by a practical lie, namely, by force. This undertaking for another, is the blunder which stands in colossal ugliness in the governments of the world. It is the same thing in numbers, as in a pair, only not quite so intelligible. I can see well enough a great difference between my setting myself down to a self-control, and my going to make somebody else act after my views: but when a quarter of the human race assume to tell me what I must do, I may be too much disturbed by the circumstances to see so clearly the absurdity of their command. Therefore, all public ends look vague and quixotic beside private ones. For, any laws but those which men make for themselves, are laughable. If I put myself in the place of my child, and we stand in one thought, and see that things are thus or thus, that perception is law for him and me. We are both there, both act. But if, without carrying him into the thought, I look over into his plot, and, guessing how it is with him, ordain this or that, he will never obey me. This is the history of governments,—one man does something which is to bind another. A man who cannot be acquainted with me, taxes me; looking from afar at me, ordains that a part of my labor shall go to this or that whimsical end, not as I, but as he happens to fancy. Behold the consequence. Of all debts, men are least willing to pay the taxes. What a satire is this on government! Everywhere they think they get their money's worth, except for these.

Hence, the less government we have, the better,—the fewer laws, and the less confided power. The antidote to this abuse of formal Government, is, the influence of private character, the growth of the Individual; the appearance of the principal to supersede the proxy;

the appearance of the wise man, of whom the existing government, is, it must be owned, but a shabby imitation. That which all things tend to educe, which freedom, cultivation, intercourse, revolutions, go to form and deliver, is character; that is the end of nature, to reach unto this coronation of her king. To educate the wise man, the State exists; and with the appearance of the wise man, the State expires. The appearance of character makes the State unnecessary. The wise man is the State. He needs no army, fort, or navy,—he loves men too well; no bribe, or feast, or palace, to draw friends to him; no vantage ground, no favorable circumstance. He needs no library, for he has not done thinking; no church, for he is a prophet; no statute book, for he has the lawgiver; no money, for he is value; no road, for he is at home where he is; no experience, for the life of the creator shoots through him, and looks from his eyes. He has no personal friends, for he who has the spell to draw the prayer and piety of all men unto him, needs not husband and educate a few, to share with him a select and poetic life. His relation to men is angelic; his memory is myrrh to them; his presence, frankincense and flowers.

We think our civilization near its meridian, but we are yet only at the cock-crowing and the morning star. In our barbarous society the influence of character is in its infancy. As a political power, as the rightful lord who is to tumble all rulers from their chairs, its presence is hardly yet suspected. Malthus and Ricardo quite omit it; the Annual Register is silent; in the Conversations' Lexicon, it is not set down; the President's Message, the Queen's Speech, have not mentioned it; and yet it is never nothing. Every thought which genius and piety throw into the world, alters the world. The gladiators in the lists of power feel, through all their frocks of force and simulation, the presence of worth. I think the very strife of trade and ambition are confession of this divinity; and successes in those fields are the poor amends, the fig-leaf with which the shamed soul attempts to hide its nakedness. I find the like unwilling homage in all quarters. It is because we know how much is due from us, that we are impatient to show some petty talent as a substitute for worth. We are haunted by a conscience of this right to grandeur of character, and are false to it. But each of us has some

talent, can do somewhat useful, or graceful, or
formidable, or amusing, or lucrative. That we
do, as an apology to others and to ourselves,
for not reaching the mark of a good and equal
life. But it does not satisfy *us*, whilst we thrust
it on the notice of our companions. It may
throw dust in their eyes, but does not smooth
our own brow, or give us the tranquillity of the
strong when we walk abroad. We do penance
as we go. Our talent is a sort of expiation, and
we are constrained to reflect on our splendid
moment, with a certain humiliation, as somewhat too fine, and not as one act of many acts,
a fair expression of our permanent energy.
Most persons of ability meet in society with a
kind of tacit appeal. Each seems to say, ' I am
not all here.' Senators and presidents have
climbed so high with pain enough, not because
they think the place specially agreeable, but as
an apology for real worth, and to vindicate
their manhood in our eyes. This conspicuous
chair is their compensation to themselves for
being of a poor, cold, hard nature. They must
do what they can. Like one class of forest animals, they have nothing but a prehensile tail:
climb they must, or crawl. If a man found

himself so rich-natured that he could enter into strict relations with the best persons, and make life serene around him by the dignity and sweetness of his behavior, could he afford to circumvent the favor of the caucus and the press, and covet relations so hollow and pompous, as those of a politician? Surely nobody would be a charlatan, who could afford to be sincere.

The tendencies of the times favor the idea of self-government, and leave the individual, for all code, to the rewards and penalties of his own constitution, which work with more energy than we believe, whilst we depend on artificial restraints. The movement in this direction has been very marked in modern history. Much has been blind and discreditable, but the nature of the revolution is not affected by the vices of the revolters ; for this is a purely moral force. It was never adopted by any party in history, neither can be. It separates the individual from all party, and unites him, at the same time, to the race. It promises a recognition of higher rights than those of personal freedom, or the security of property. A man has a right to be employed, to be trusted, to be loved, to be revered. The power of love, as the basis of a State, has never been tried. We must not imagine that all things are lapsing into confusion, if every tender protestant be not compelled to bear his part in certain social conventions : nor doubt that roads can be built, letters carried, and the fruit of labor secured, when the government of force is at an end. Are our methods now so excellent that all competition is hopeless ? Could not a nation of friends even devise better ways ? On the other hand, let not the most conservative and timid fear anything from a premature surrender of the bayonet, and the system of force. For, according to the order of nature, which is quite superior to our will, it stands thus ; there will always be a government of force, where men are selfish ; and when they are pure enough to abjure the code of force, they will be wise enough to see how these public ends of the post-office, of the highway, of commerce, and the exchange of property, of museums and libraries, of institutions of art and science, can be answered.

We live in a very low state of the world, and pay unwilling tribute to governments founded on force. There is not, among the most religious and instructed men of the most religious

and civil nations, a reliance on the moral sentiment, and a sufficient belief in the unity of
things to persuade them that society can be
maintained without artificial restraints, as well
as the solar system; or that the private citizen
might be reasonable, and a good neighbor, without the hint of a jail or a confiscation. What is
strange too, there never was in any man sufficient faith in the power of rectitude, to inspire
him with the broad design of renovating the
State on the principle of right and love. All
those who have pretended this design, have been
partial reformers, and have admitted in some
manner the supremacy of the bad State. I do
not call to mind a single human being who has
steadily denied the authority of the laws, on
the simple ground of his own moral nature.
Such designs, full of genius and full of fate as
they are, are not entertained except avowedly
as air-pictures. If the individual who exhibits
them, dare to think them practicable, he dis-
gusts scholars and churchmen; and men of
talent, and women of superior sentiments, cannot hide their contempt. Not the less does
nature continue to fill the heart of youth with
suggestions of this enthusiasm, and there are

now men,—if indeed I can speak in the plural number,—more exactly, I will say, I have just been conversing with one man, to whom no weight of adverse experience will make it for a moment appear impossible, that thousands of human beings might exercise towards each other the grandest and simplest sentiments, as well as a knot of friends, or a pair of lovers.

NOMINALIST AND REALIST.

In countless upward-striving waves
The moon-drawn tide-wave strives;
In thousand far-transplanted grafts
The parent fruit survives;
So, in the new-born millions,
The perfect Adam lives.
Not less are summer-mornings dear
To every child they wake,
And each with novel life his sphere
Fills for his proper sake.

(241)

ESSAY VIII.

NOMINALIST AND REALIST.

I CANNOT often enough say, that a man is only a relative and representative nature. Each is a hint of the truth, but far enough from being that truth, which yet he quite newly and inevitably suggests to us. If I seek it in him, I shall not find it. Could any man conduct into me the pure stream of that which he pretends to be! Long afterwards, I find that quality elsewhere which he promised me. The genius of the Platonists, is intoxicating to the student, yet how few particulars of it can I detach from all their books. The man momentarily stands for the thought, but will not bear examination; and a society of men will cursorily represent well enough a certain quality and culture, for example, chivalry or beauty of manners, but separate them, and there is no gentleman and no lady in the group. The least hint sets us on the pursuit of a character, which no man

(243)

realizes. We have such exorbitant eyes, that on seeing the smallest arc, we complete the curve, and when the curtain is lifted from the diagram which it seemed to veil, we are vexed to find that no more was drawn, than just that fragment of an arc which we first beheld. We are greatly too liberal in our construction of each other's faculty and promise. Exactly what the parties have already done, they shall do again; but that which we inferred from their nature and inception, they will not do. That is in nature, but not in them. That happens in the world, which we often witness in a public debate. Each of the speakers expresses himself imperfectly: no one of them hears much that another says, such is the preoccupation of mind of each; and the audience, who have only to hear and not to speak, judge very wisely and superiorly how wrongheaded and unskilful is each of the debaters to his own affair. Great men or men of great gifts you shall easily find, but symmetrical men never. When I meet a pure intellectual force, or a generosity of affection, I believe, here then is man; and am presently mortified by the discovery, that this individual is no more available to his own or to the general ends, than his companions; because the power which drew my respect, is not supported by the total symphony of his talents. All persons exist to society by some shining trait of beauty or utility, which they have. We borrow the proportions of the man from that one fine feature, and finish the portrait symmetrically; which is false; for the rest of his body is small or deformed. I observe a person who makes a good public appearance, and conclude thence the perfection of his private character, on which this is based; but he has no private character. He is a graceful cloak or lay-figure for holidays. All our poets, heroes, and saints, fail utterly in some one or in many parts to satisfy our idea, fail to draw our spontaneous interest, and so leave us without any hope of realization but in our own future. Our exaggeration of all fine characters arises from the fact, that we identify each in turn with the soul. But there are no such men as we fable; no Jesus, nor Pericles, nor Cæsar, nor Angelo, nor Washington, such as we have made. We consecrate a great deal of nonsense, because it was allowed by great men. There is none without his foible. I verily believe if an angel should come to chaunt the chorus of the moral law, he would eat too much gingerbread, or take liberties with private letters, or do some precious atrocity. It is bad enough, that our geniuses cannot do anything useful, but it is worse that no man is fit for society, who has fine traits. He is admired at a distance, but he cannot come near without appearing a cripple. The men of fine parts protect themselves by solitude, or by courtesy, or by satire, or by an acid worldly manner, each concealing, as he best can, his incapacity for useful association, but they want either love or self-reliance.

Our native love of reality joins with this experience to teach us a little reserve, and to dissuade a too sudden surrender to the brilliant qualities of persons. Young people admire talents or particular excellences; as we grow older, we value total powers and effects, as, the impression, the quality, the spirit of men and things. The genius is all. The man,—it is his system : we do not try a solitary word or act, but his habit. The acts which you praise, I praise not, since they are departures from his faith, and are mere compliances. The magnetism which arranges tribes and races in one polarity, is alone to be respected; the men are steel-filings. Yet we unjustly select a particle, and say, 'O steel-filing number one! what heart-drawings I feel to thee! what prodigious virtues are these of thine! how constitutional to thee, and incommunicable.' Whilst we speak, the loadstone is withdrawn; down falls our filing in a heap with the rest, and we continue our mummery to the wretched shaving. Let us go for universals; for the magnetism, not for the needles. Human life and its persons are poor empirical pretensions. A personal influence is an *ignis fatuus*. If they say, it is great, it is great; if they say, it is small, it is small; you see it, and you see it not, by turns; it borrows all its size from the momentary estimation of the speakers : the Will-of-the-wisp vanishes, if you go too near, vanishes if you go too far, and only blazes at one angle. Who can tell if Washington be a great man, or no? Who can tell if Franklin be? Yes, or any but the twelve, or six, or three great gods of fame? And they, too, loom and fade before the eternal.

We are amphibious creatures, weaponed for two elements, having two sets of faculties, the particular and the catholic. We adjust our instrument for general observation, and sweep the heavens as easily as we pick out a single figure in the terrestrial landscape. We are practically skilful in detecting elements, for which we have no place in our theory, and no name. Thus we are very sensible of an atmospheric influence in men and in bodies of men, not accounted for in an arithmetical addition of all their measurable properties. There is a genius of a nation, which is not to be found in the numerical citizens, but which characterizes the society. England, strong, punctual, practical, well-spoken England, I should not find, if I should go to the island to seek it. In the parliament, in the playhouse, at dinner-tables, I might see a great number of rich, ignorant, book-read, conventional, proud men, —many old women,—and not anywhere the Englishman who made the good speeches, combined the accurate engines, and did the bold and nervous deeds. It is even worse in America, where, from the intellectual quickness of the race, the genius of the country is more splendid in its promise, and more slight in its performance. Webster cannot do the work of Webster. We conceive distinctly enough the

French, the Spanish, the German genius, and it is not the less real, that perhaps we should not meet in either of those nations, a single individual who corresponded with the type. We infer the spirit of the nation in great measure from the language, which is a sort of monument, to which each forcible individual in a course of many hundred years has contributed a stone. And, universally, a good example of this social force, is the veracity of language, which cannot be debauched. In any controversy concerning morals, an appeal may be made with safety to the sentiments, which the language of the people expresses. Proverbs, words, and grammar inflections convey the public sense with more purity and precision, than the wisest individual.

In the famous dispute with the Nominalists, the Realists had a good deal of reason. General ideas are essences. They are our gods: they round and ennoble the most partial and sordid way of living. Our proclivity to details cannot quite degrade our life, and divest it of poetry. The day-laborer is reckoned as standing at the foot of the social scale, yet he is saturated with the laws of the world. His meas-

ures are the hours; morning and night, solstice
and equinox, geometry, astronomy, and all the
lovely accidents of nature play through his mind.
Money, which represents the prose of life, and
which is hardly spoken of in parlors without an
apology, is, in its effects and laws, as beautiful
as roses. Property keeps the accounts of the
world, and is always moral. The property will
be found where the labor, the wisdom, and the
virtue have been in nations, in classes, and (the
whole life-time considered, with the compensa-
tions) in the individual also. How wise the
world appears, when the laws and usages of
nations are largely detailed, and the completeness of the municipal system is considered!
Nothing is left out. If you go into the markets,
and the custom-houses, the insurers' and nota-
ries' offices, the offices of sealers of weights and
measures, of inspection of provisions,—it will
appear as if one man had made it all. Wherever you go, a wit like your own has been before
you, and has realized its thought. The Eleu-
sinian mysteries, the Egyptian architecture, the
Indian astronomy, the Greek sculpture, show
that there always were seeing and knowing men
in the planet. The world is full of masonic ties,

of guilds, of secret and public legions of honor;
that of scholars, for example ; and that of gentlemen fraternizing with the upper class of
every country and every culture.

I am very much struck in literature by the
appearance, that one person wrote all the books ;
as if the editor of a journal planted his body of
reporters in different parts of the field of action,
and relieved some by others from time to time ;
but there is such equality and identity both of
judgment and point of view in the narrative,
that it is plainly the work of one all-seeing, all-
hearing gentleman.   I looked into Pope's Odys-
sey yesterday : it is as correct and elegant after
our canon of today, as if it were newly written.
The modernness of all good books seems to
give me an existence as wide as man.   What is
well done, I feel as if I did ; what is ill-done, I
reck not of.   Shakspeare's passages of passion
(for example, in Lear and Hamlet) are in the
very dialect of the present year.   I am faithful
again to the whole over the members in my use
of books.   I find the most pleasure in reading a
book in a manner least flattering to the author.
I read Proclus, and sometimes Plato, as I might
read a dictionary, for a mechanical help to the

fancy and the imagination. I read for the lustres, as if one should use a fine picture in a chromatic experiment, for its rich colors. 'Tis not Proclus, but a piece of nature and fate that I explore. It is a greater joy to see the author's author, than himself. A higher pleasure of the same kind I found lately at a concert, where I went to hear Handel's Messiah. As the master overpowered the littleness and incapableness of the performers, and made them conductors of his electricity, so it was easy to observe what efforts nature was making through so many hoarse, wooden, and imperfect persons, to produce beautiful voices, fluid and soul-guided men and women. The genius of nature was paramount at the oratorio.

This preference of the genius to the parts is the secret of that deification of art, which is found in all superior minds. Art, in the artist, is proportion, or, a habitual respect to the whole by an eye loving beauty in details. And the wonder and charm of it is the sanity in insanity which it denotes. Proportion is almost impossible to human beings. There is no one who does not exaggerate. In conversation, men are encumbered with personality, and talk too much.

In modern sculpture, picture, and poetry, the beauty is miscellaneous; the artist works here and there, and at all points, adding and adding, instead of unfolding the unit of his thought. Beautiful details we must have, or no artist: but they must be means and never other. The eye must not lose sight for a moment of the purpose. Lively boys write to their ear and eye, and the cool reader finds nothing but sweet jingles in it. When they grow older, they respect the argument.

We obey the same intellectual integrity, when we study in exceptions the law of the world. Anomalous facts, as the never quite obsolete rumors of magic and demonology, and the new allegations of phrenologists and neurologists, are of ideal use. They are good indications. Homœopathy is insignificant as an art of healing, but of great value as criticism on the hygeia or medical practice of the time. So with Mesmerism, Swedenborgism, Fourierism, and the Millennial Church; they are poor pretensions enough, but good criticism on the science, philosophy, and preaching of the day. For these abnormal insights of the adepts, ought to be normal, and things of course.

All things show us, that on every side we are very near to the best. It seems not worth while to execute with too much pains some one intellectual, or æsthetical, or civil feat, when presently the dream will scatter, and we shall burst into universal power. The reason of idleness and of crime is the deferring of our hopes. Whilst we are waiting, we beguile the time with jokes, with sleep, with eating, and with crimes.

Thus we settle it in our cool libraries, that all the agents with which we deal are subalterns, which we can well afford to let pass, and life will be simpler when we live at the centre, and flout the surfaces. I wish to speak with all respect of persons, but sometimes I must pinch myself to keep awake, and preserve the due decorum. They melt so fast into each other, that they are like grass and trees, and it needs an effort to treat them as individuals. Though the uninspired man certainly finds persons a conveniency in household matters, the divine man does not respect them: he sees them as a rack of clouds, or a fleet of ripples which the wind drives over the surface of the water. But this is flat rebellion. Nature will not be Buddhist: she resents generalizing, and insults the philosopher in every moment with a million of fresh particulars. It is all idle talking: as much as a man is a whole, so is he also a part; and it were partial not to see it. What you say in your pompous distribution only distributes you into your class and section. You have not got rid of parts by denying them, but are the more partial. You are one thing, but nature is *one thing and the other thing*, in the same moment. She will not remain orbed in a thought, but rushes into persons; and when each person, inflamed to a fury of personality, would conquer all things to his poor crotchet, she raises up against him another person, and by many persons incarnates again a sort of whole. She will have all. Nick Bottom cannot play all the parts, work it how he may: there will be somebody else, and the world will be round. Everything must have its flower or effort at the beautiful, coarser or finer according to its stuff. They relieve and recommend each other, and the sanity of society is a balance of a thousand insanities. She punishes abstractionists, and will only forgive an induction which is rare and casual. We like to come to a height of land and see the landscape, just as we value a general remark in conversation. But it is not the intention of nature that we should live by general views. We fetch fire and water, run about all day among the shops and markets, and get our clothes and shoes made and mended, and are the victims of these details, and once in a fortnight we arrive perhaps at a rational moment. If we were not thus infatuated, if we saw the real from hour to hour, we should not be here to write and to read, but should have been burned or frozen long ago. She would never get anything done, if she suffered admirable Crichtons, and universal geniuses. She loves better a wheelwright who dreams all night of wheels, and a groom who is part of his horse: for she is full of work, and these are her hands. As the frugal farmer takes care that his cattle shall eat down the rowan, and swine shall eat the waste of his house, and poultry shall pick the crumbs, so our economical mother despatches a new genius and habit of mind into every district and condition of existence, plants an eye wherever a new ray of light can fall, and gathering up into some man every property in

the universe, establishes thousandfold occult
mutual attractions among her offspring, that all
this wash and waste of power may be imparted
and exchanged.

Great dangers undoubtedly accrue from this
incarnation and distribution of the godhead,
and hence nature has her maligners, as if she
were Circe; and Alphonso of Castille fancied
he could have given useful advice. But she
does not go unprovided; she has hellebore at
the bottom of the cup. Solitude would ripen
a plentiful crop of despots. The recluse thinks
of men as having his manner, or as not having
his manner; and as having degrees of it, more
and less. But when he comes into a public
assembly, he sees that men have very different
manners from his own, and in their way admirable. In his childhood and youth, he has had
many checks and censures, and thinks modestly
enough of his own endowment. When afterwards he comes to unfold it in propitious circumstance, it seems the only talent: he is delighted with his success, and accounts himself
already the fellow of the great. But he goes
into a mob, into a banking-house, into a me-
chanic's shop, into a mill, into a laboratory, into
42

a ship, into a camp, and in each new place he is no better than an idiot: other talents take place, and rule the hour. The rotation which whirls every leaf and pebble to the meridian, reaches to every gift of man, and we all take turns at the top.

For nature, who abhors mannerism, has set her heart on breaking up all styles and tricks, and it is so much easier to do what one has done before, than to do a new thing, that there is a perpetual tendency to a set mode. In every conversation, even the highest, there is a certain trick, which may be soon learned by an acute person, and then that particular style continued indefinitely. Each man, too, is a tyrant in tendency, because he would impose his idea on others; and their trick is their natural defence. Jesus would absorb the race; but Tom Paine or the coarsest blasphemer helps humanity by resisting this exuberance of power. Hence the immense benefit of party in politics, as it reveals faults of character in a chief, which the intellectual force of the persons, with or-dinary opportunity, and not hurled into aphelion by hatred, could not have seen. Since we are all so stupid, what benefit that there should be two stupidities! It is like that brute advantage so essential to astronomy, of having the diameter of the earth's orbit for a base of its triangles. Democracy is morose, and runs to anarchy, but in the state, and in the schools, it is indispensable to resist the consolidation of all men into a few men. If John was perfect, why are you and I alive? As long as any man exists, there is some need of him; let him fight for his own. A new poet has appeared; a new character approached us; why should we refuse to eat bread, until we have found his regiment and section in our old army-files? Why not a new man? Here is a new enterprise of Brook Farm, of Skeneateles, of Northampton: why so impatient to baptise them Essenes, or Port-Royalists, or Shakers, or by any known and effete name? Let it be a new way of living. Why have only two or three ways of life, and not thousands? Every man is wanted, and no man is wanted much. We came this time for condiments, not for corn. We want the great genius only for joy; for one star more in our constellation, for one tree more in our grove. But he thinks we wish to belong to him, as he wishes to occupy us. He greatly mistakes us.

I think I have done well, if I have acquired a new word from a good author; and my business with him is to find my own, though it were only to melt him down into an epithet or an image for daily use.

> "Into paint will I grind thee, my bride!"

To embroil the confusion, and make it impossible to arrive at any general statement, when we have insisted on the imperfection of individuals, our affections and our experience urge that every individual is entitled to honor, and a very generous treatment is sure to be repaid. A recluse sees only two or three persons, and allows them all their room; they spread themselves at large. The man of state looks at many, and compares the few habitually with others, and these look less. Yet are they not entitled to this generosity of reception? and is not munificence the means of insight? For though gamesters say, that the cards beat all the players, though they were never so skilful, yet in the contest we are now considering, the players are also the game, and share the power of the cards. If you criticise a fine genius, the odds are that you are out of your reckoning, and, instead of the poet, are censuring your own caricature of him. For there is somewhat spheral and infinite in every man, especially in every genius, which, if you can come very near him, sports with all your limitations. For, rightly, every man is a channel through which heaven floweth, and, whilst I fancied I was criticising him, I was censuring or rather terminating my own soul. After taxing Goethe as a courtier, artificial, unbelieving, worldly,—I took up this book of Helena, and found him an Indian of the wilderness, a piece of pure nature like an apple or an oak, large as morning or night, and virtuous as a briar-rose.

But care is taken that the whole tune shall be played. If we were not kept among surfaces, every thing would be large and universal : now the excluded attributes burst in on us with the more brightness, that they have been excluded. " Your turn now, my turn next," is the rule of the game. The universality being hindered in its primary form, comes in the secondary form of *all sides :* the points come in succession to the meridian, and by the speed of rotation, a new whole is formed. Nature keeps herself whole, and her representation complete

in the experience of each mind. She suffers
no seat to be vacant in her college. It is the
secret of the world that all things subsist, and do
not die, but only retire a little from sight, and
afterwards return again. Whatever does not
concern us, is concealed from us. As soon as
a person is no longer related to our present
well-being, he is concealed, or *dies*, as we say.
Really, all things and persons are related to us,
but according to our nature, they act on us not
at once, but in succession, and we are made
aware of their presence one at a time. All
persons, all things which we have known, are
here present, and many more than we see; the
world is full. As the ancient said, the world is
a *plenum* or solid; and if we saw all things that
really surround us, we should be imprisoned
and unable to move. For, though nothing is
impassable to the soul, but all things are per-
vious to it, and like highways, yet this is only
whilst the soul does not see them. As soon as
the soul sees any object, it stops before that object. Therefore, the divine Providence, which
keeps the universe open in every direction to
the soul, conceals all the furniture and all the
persons that do not concern a particular soul.

from the senses of that individual. Through solidest eternal things, the man finds his road, as if they did not subsist, and does not once suspect their being. As soon as he needs a new object, suddenly he beholds it, and no longer attempts to pass through it, but takes another way. When he has exhausted for the time the nourishment to be drawn from any one person or thing, that object is withdrawn from his observation, and though still in his immediate neighborhood, he does not suspect its presence.

Nothing is dead: men feign themselves dead, and endure mock funerals and mournful obituaries, and there they stand looking out of the window, sound and well, in some new and strange disguise. Jesus is not dead: he is very well alive: nor John, nor Paul, nor Mahomet, nor Aristotle; at times we believe we have seen them all, and could easily tell the names under which they go.

If we cannot make voluntary and conscious steps in the admirable science of universals, let us see the parts wisely, and infer the genius of nature from the best particulars with a becoming charity. What is best in each kind is an index of what should be the average of that thing. Love shows me the opulence of nature, by disclosing to me in my friend a hidden wealth, and I infer an equal depth of good in every other direction. It is commonly said by farmers, that a good pear or apple costs no more time or pains to rear, than a poor one; so I would have no work of art, no speech, or action, or thought, or friend, but the best.

The end and the means, the gamester and the game,—life is made up of the intermixture and reaction of these two amicable powers, whose marriage appears beforehand monstrous, as each denies and tends to abolish the other. We must reconcile the contradictions as we can, but their discord and their concord introduce wild absurdities into our thinking and speech. No sentence will hold the whole truth, and the only way in which we can be just, is by giving ourselves the lie; Speech is better than silence; silence is better than speech;—All things are in contact; every atom has a sphere of repulsion;—Things are, and are not, at the same time;—and the like. All the universe over, there is but one thing, this old Two-Face, creator-creature, mind-matter, right-wrong, of

which any proposition may be affirmed or
denied.   Very fitly, therefore, I assert, that
every man is a partialist, that nature secures
him as an instrument by self-conceit, preventing
the tendencies to religion and science; and now
further assert, that, each man's genius being
nearly and affectionately explored, he is justi-
fied in his individuality, as his nature is found
to be immense; and now I add, that every man
is a universalist also, and, as our earth, whilst it
spins on its own axis, spins all the time around
the sun through the celestial spaces, so the
least of its rational children, the most dedicated
to his private affair, works out, though as it
were under a disguise, the universal problem.
We fancy men are individuals; so are pump-
kins; but every pumpkin in the field, goes
through every point of pumpkin history.   The
rabid democrat, as soon as he is senator and
rich man, has ripened beyond possibility of
sincere radicalism, and unless he can resist the
sun, he must be conservative the remainder
of his days.   Lord Eldon said in his old age,
" that, if he were to begin life again, he would
be damned but he would begin as agitator."

We hide this universality, if we can, but it

appears at all points.   We are as ungrateful as
children.   There is nothing we cherish and
strive to draw to us, but in some hour we turn
and rend it.   We keep a running fire of sar-
casm at ignorance and the life of the senses;
then goes by, perchance, a fair girl, a piece of
life, gay and happy, and making the commonest offices beautiful, by the energy and heart
with which she does them, and seeing this,
we admire and love her and them, and say,
" Lo! a genuine creature of the fair earth, not
dissipated, or too early ripened by books, philosophy, religion, society, or care! " insinuating
a treachery and contempt for all we had so
long loved and wrought in ourselves and
others.

If we could have any security against moods!
If the profoundest prophet could be holden to
his words, and the hearer who is ready to sell
all and join the crusade, could have any certificate that to-morrow his prophet shall not unsay
his testimony!   But the Truth sits veiled there
on the Bench, and never interposes an adamantine syllable; and the most sincere and revo-
lutionary doctrine, put as if the ark of God
were carried forward some furlongs, and planted

there for the succor of the world, shall in a few
weeks be coldly set aside by the same speaker,
as morbid; "I thought I was right, but I was
not,"—and the same immeasurable credulity
demanded for new audacities. If we were not
of all opinions! if we did not in any moment
shift the platform on which we stand, and look
and speak from another! if there could be any
regulation, any 'one-hour-rule,' that a man
should never leave his point of view, without
sound of trumpet. I am always insincere, as
always knowing there are other moods.

How sincere and confidential we can be, saying all that lies in the mind, and yet go away
feeling that all is yet unsaid, from the incapacity
of the parties to know each other, although
they use the same words! My companion assumes to know my mood and habit of thought,
and we go on from explanation to explanation,
until all is said which words can, and we leave
matters just as they were at first, because of
that vicious assumption. Is it that every man
believes every other to be an incurable partialist,
and himself an universalist? I talked yesterday with a pair of philosophers: I endeavored
to show my good men that I love everything

by turns, and nothing long; that I loved the centre, but doated on the superficies; that I loved man, if men seemed to me mice and rats; that I revered saints, but woke up glad that the old pagan world stood its ground, and died hard; that I was glad of men of every gift and nobility, but would not live in their arms. Could they but once understand, that I loved to know that they existed, and heartily wished them Godspeed, yet, out of my poverty of life and thought, had no word or welcome for them when they came to see me, and could well consent to their living in Oregon, for any claim I felt on them, it would be a great satis-faction.

NEW ENGLAND REFORMERS.

NEW ENGLAND REFORMERS.

———

A LECTURE READ BEFORE THE SOCIETY IN AMORY HALL, ON SUNDAY, 3 MARCH, 1844.

WHOEVER has had opportunity of acquaintance with society in New England, during the last twenty-five years, with those middle and with those leading sections that may constitute any just representation of the character and aim of the community, will have been struck with the great activity of thought and experimenting. His attention must be commanded by the signs that the Church, or religious party, is falling from the church nominal, and is appearing in temperance and non-resistance societies, in movements of abolitionists and of socialists, and in very significant assemblies, called Sabbath and Bible Conventions,—composed of ultraists, of seekers, of all the soul of the soldiery of dissent, and meeting to call in question the authority of the Sabbath, of the priesthood, and of the church. In these movements, nothing was

(271)

more remarkable than the discontent they begot
in the movers. The spirit of protest and of detachment, drove the members of these Conventions to bear testimony against the church, and
immediately afterward, to declare their discontent with these Conventions, their independence
of their colleagues, and their impatience of the
methods whereby they were working. They
defied each other, like a congress of kings,
each of whom had a realm to rule, and a way
of his own that made concert unprofitable.
What a fertility of projects for the salvation of
the world! One apostle thought all men should
go to farming; and another, that no man should
buy or sell: that the use of money was the
cardinal evil; another, that the mischief was in
our diet, that we eat and drink damnation.
These made unleavened bread, and were foes to
the death to fermentation. It was in vain urged
by the housewife, that God made yeast, as well
as dough, and loves fermentation just as dearly
as he loves vegetation; that fermentation
develops the saccharine element in the grain,
and makes it more palatable and more digesti-
ble. No; they wish the pure wheat, and will
die but it shall not ferment. Stop, dear nature,

these incessant advances of thine; let us scotch these ever-rolling wheels! Others attacked the system of agriculture, the use of animal manures in farming; and the tyranny of man over brute nature; these abuses polluted his food. The ox must be taken from the plough, and the horse from the cart, the hundred acres of the farm must be spaded, and the man must walk wherever boats and locomotives will not carry him. Even the insect world was to be defended,—that had been too long neglected, and a society for the protection of ground-worms, slugs, and mosquitos was to be incorporated without delay. With these appeared the adepts of homœopathy, of hydropathy, of mesmerism, of phrenology, and their wonderful theories of the Christian miracles! Others assailed particular vocations, as that of the lawyer, that of the merchant, of the manufacturer, of the clergyman, of the scholar. Others attacked the institution of marriage, as the fountain of social evils. Others devoted themselves to the worrying of churches and meetings for public worship; and the fertile forms of antinomianism among the elder puritans, seemed to have their match in the plenty of the new harvest of reform.

43

With this din of opinion and debate, there was a keener scrutiny of institutions and domestic life than any we had known, there was sincere protesting against existing evils, and there were changes of employment dictated by conscience. No doubt, there was plentiful vaporing, and cases of backsliding might occur. But in each of these movements emerged a good result, a tendency to the adoption of simpler methods, and an assertion of the sufficiency of the private man. Thus it was directly in the spirit and genius of the age, what happened in one instance, when a church censured and threatened to excommunicate one of its members, on account of the somewhat hostile part to the church, which his conscience led him to take in the anti-slavery business; the threatened individual immediately excommunicated the church in a public and formal process. This has been several times repeated: it was excellent when it was done the first time, but, of course, loses all value when it is copied. Every project in the history of reform, no matter how violent and surprising, is good, when it is the dictate of a man's genius and constitution, but very dull and suspicious when adopted from

another.   It is right and beautiful in any man to
say, 'I will take this coat, or this book, or this
measure of corn of yours,'—in whom we see the
act to be original, and to flow from the whole
spirit and faith of him; for then that taking will
have a giving as free and divine: but we are
very easily disposed to resist the same generosity of speech, when we miss originality and
truth to character in it.

There was in all the practical activities of
New England, for the last quarter of a century,
a gradual withdrawal of tender consciences from
the social organizations.   There is observable
throughout, the contest between mechanical
and spiritual methods, but with a steady tendency of the thoughtful and virtuous to a deeper
belief and reliance on spiritual facts.

In politics, for example, it is easy to see the
progress of dissent.   The country is full of rebellion; the country is full of kings.   Hands
off! let there be no control and no interference
in the administration of the affairs of this kingdom of me.   Hence the growth of the doctrine
and of the party of Free Trade, and the willingness to try that experiment, in the face of what
appear incontestable facts.   I confess, the motto

of the Globe newspaper is so attractive to me, that I can seldom find much appetite to read what is below it in its columns, "The world is governed too much." So the country is frequently affording solitary examples of resistance to the government, solitary nullifiers, who throw themselves on their reserved rights; nay, who have reserved all their rights; who reply to the assessor, and to the clerk of court, that they do not know the State; and embarrass the courts of law, by non-juring, and the commander-in-chief of the militia, by non-resistance.

The same disposition to scrutiny and dissent appeared in civil, festive, neighborly, and domestic society. A restless, prying, conscientious criticism broke out in unexpected quarters. Who gave me the money with which I bought my coat? Why should professional labor and that of the counting-house be paid so disproportionately to the labor of the porter, and wood-sawyer? This whole business of Trade gives me to pause and think, as it constitutes false relations between men; inasmuch as I am prone to count myself relieved of any responsibility to behave well and nobly to that person whom I pay with money, whereas if I had not that commodity, I should be put on my good behavior in all companies, and man would be a benefactor to man, as being himself his only certificate that he had a right to those aids and services which each asked of the other. Am I not too protected a person? is there not a wide disparity between the lot of me and the lot of thee, my poor brother, my poor sister? Am I not defrauded of my best culture in the loss of those gymnastics which manual labor and the emergencies of poverty constitute? I find nothing healthful or exalting in the smooth conventions of society; I do not like the close air of saloons. I begin to suspect myself to be a prisoner, though treated with all this courtesy and luxury. I pay a destructive tax in my conformity.

The same insatiable criticism may be traced in the efforts for the reform of Education. The popular education has been taxed with a want of truth and nature. It was complained that an education to things was not given. We are students of words : we are shut up in schools, and colleges, and recitation-rooms, for ten or fifteen years, and come out at last with a bag of wind, a memory of words, and do not know a thing. We cannot use our hands, or our legs, or our eyes, or our arms. We do not know an edible root in the woods, we cannot tell our course by the stars, nor the hour of the day by the sun. It is well if we can swim and skate. We are afraid of a horse, of a cow, of a dog, of a snake, of a spider. The Roman rule was, to teach a boy nothing that he could not learn standing. The old English rule was, 'All summer in the field, and all winter in the study.' And it seems as if a man should learn to plant, or to fish, or to hunt, that he might secure his subsistence at all events, and not be painful to his friends and fellow men. The lessons of science should be experimental also. The sight of the planet through a telescope, is worth all the course on astronomy: the shock of the electric spark in the elbow, out-values all the theories; the taste of the nitrous oxide, the firing of an artificial volcano, are better than volumes of chemistry.

One of the traits of the new spirit, is the inquisition it fixed on our scholastic devotion to the dead languages. The ancient languages, with great beauty of structure, contain wonderful remains of genius, which draw, and always will draw, certain likeminded men,—Greek men, and Roman men, in all countries, to their study; but by a wonderful drowsiness of usage, they had exacted the study of *all* men. Once (say two centuries ago), Latin and Greek had a strict relation to all the science and culture there was in Europe, and the Mathematics had a momentary importance at some era of activity in physical science. These things became stereotyped as *education*, as the manner of men is. But the Good Spirit never cared for the colleges, and though all men and boys were now drilled in Latin, Greek, and Mathematics, it had quite left these shells high and dry on the beach, and was now creating and feeding other matters at other ends of the world. But in a hundred high schools and colleges, this warfare against common sense still goes on. Four, or six, or ten years, the pupil is parsing Greek and Latin, and as soon as he leaves the University, as it is ludicrously called, he shuts those books for the last time. Some thousands of young men are graduated at our colleges in this country every year, and the persons who, at forty years, still read Greek, can all be counted on your hand. I never met with ten. Four or five persons I have seen who read Plato.

But is not this absurd, that the whole liberal
talent of this country should be directed in its
best years on studies which lead to nothing?
What was the consequence? Some intelligent
person said or thought: 'Is that Greek and
Latin some spell to conjure with, and not words
of reason? If the physician, the lawyer, the
divine, never use it to come at their ends, I
need never learn it to come at mine. Conjur-
ing is gone out of fashion, and I will omit this
conjugating, and go straight to affairs.' So
they jumped the Greek and Latin, and read
law, medicine, or sermons, without it. To the
astonishment of all, the self-made men took
even ground at once with the oldest of the reg-
ular graduates, and in a few months the most
conservative circles of Boston and New York
had quite forgotten who of their gownsmen was
college-bred, and who was not.

One tendency appears alike in the philosophical speculation, and in the rudest demo-
cratical movements, through all the petulance
and all the puerility, the wish, namely, to cast
aside the superfluous, and arrive at short methods,
urged, as I suppose, by an intuition that the
human spirit is equal to all emergencies, alone,

and that man is more often injured than helped
by the means he uses.

I conceive this gradual casting off of material
aids, and the indication of growing trust in the
private, self-supplied powers of the individual,
to be the affirmative principle of the recent philosophy : and that it is feeling its own profound
truth, and is reaching forward at this very hour
to the happiest conclusions.   I readily concede
that in this, as in every period of intellectual
activity, there has been a noise of denial and
protest ; much was to be resisted, much was to
be got rid of by those who were reared in the
old, before they could begin to affirm and to
construct.   Many a reformer perishes in his
removal of rubbish,—and that makes the offen-
siveness of the class.   They are partial; they
are not equal to the work they pretend.   They
lose their way ; in the assault on the kingdom
of darkness, they expend all their energy on
some accidental evil, and lose their sanity and
power of benefit.   It is of little moment that one
or two, or twenty errors of our social system be
corrected, but of much that the man be in his
senses.

The   criticism   and   attack   on   institutions

which we have witnessed, has made one thing
plain, that society gains nothing whilst a man,
not himself renovated, attempts to renovate
things around him : he has become tediously
good in some particular, but negligent or narrow in the rest; and hypocrisy and vanity are
often the disgusting result.

It is handsomer to remain in the establishment better than the establishment, and conduct
that in the best manner, than to make a sally
against evil by some single improvement, without supporting it by a total regeneration.   Do
not be so vain of your one objection.   Do you
think there is only one ? Alas ! my good friend,
there is no part of society or of life better than
any other part.   All our things are right and
wrong together.   The wave of evil washes all
our institutions alike.   Do you complain of our
Marriage ?   Our marriage is no worse than our
education, our diet, our trade, our social customs.   Do you complain of the laws of Property ?   It is a pedantry to give such importance to them.   Can we not play the game of
life with these counters, as well as with those;
in the institution of property, as well as out of
it.   Let into it the new and renewing principle

of love, and property will be universality. No one gives the impression of superiority to the institution, which he must give who will reform it. It makes no difference what you say: you must make me feel that you are aloof from it; by your natural and supernatural advantages, do easily see to the end of it,—do see how man can do without it. Now all men are on one side. No man deserves to be heard against property. Only Love, only an Idea, is against property, as we hold it.

I cannot afford to be irritable and captious, nor to waste all my time in attacks. If I should go out of church whenever I hear a false sentiment, I could never stay there five minutes. But why come out? the street is as false as the church, and when I get to my house, or to my manners, or to my speech, I have not got away from the lie. When we see an eager assailant of one of these wrongs, a special reformer, we feel like asking him, What right have you, sir, to your one virtue? Is virtue piecemeal? This is a jewel amidst the rags of a beggar.

In another way the right will be vindicated. In the midst of abuses, in the heart of cities, in the aisles of false churches, alike in one place and in another,—wherever, namely, a just and heroic soul finds itself, there it will do what is next at hand, and by the new quality of character it shall put forth, it shall abrogate that old condition, law or school in which it stands, before the law of its own mind.

If partiality was one fault of the movement party, the other defect was their reliance on Association. Doubts such as those I have intimated, drove many good persons to agitate the questions of social reform. But the revolt against the spirit of commerce, the spirit of aristocracy, and the inveterate abuses of cities, did not appear possible to individuals; and to do battle against numbers, they armed themselves with numbers, and against concert, they relied on new concert.

Following, or advancing beyond the ideas of St. Simon, of Fourier, and of Owen, three communities have already been formed in Massachusetts on kindred plans, and many more in the country at large. They aim to give every member a share in the manual labor, to give an equal reward to labor and to talent, and to unite a liberal culture with an education to labor. The scheme offers, by the economies of associated labor and expense, to make every member rich, on the same amount of property, that, in separate families, would leave every member poor. These new associations are composed of men and women of superior talents and sentiments: yet it may easily be questioned, whether such a community will draw, except in its beginnings, the able and the good; whether those who have energy, will not prefer their chance of superiority and power in the world, to the humble certainties of the Association; whether such a retreat does not promise to become an asylum to those who have tried and failed, rather than a field to the strong; and whether the members will not necessarily be fractions of men, because each finds that he cannot enter it, without some compromise. Friendship and association are very fine things, and a grand phalanx of the best of the human race, banded for some catholic object: yes, excellent; but remember that no society can ever be so large as one man. He in his friendship, in his natural and momentary associations, doubles or multiplies himself; but in the hour in which he mortgages himself to two or ten or twenty, he dwarfs himself below the stature of one.

But the men of less faith could not thus believe, and to such, concert appears the sole specific of strength.   I have failed, and you have
failed, but perhaps together we shall not fail.
Our housekeeping is not satisfactory to us, but
perhaps a phalanx, a community, might be.
Many of us have differed in opinion, and we
could find no man who could make the truth
plain, but possibly a college, or an ecclesiastical
council might.   I have not been able either to
persuade my brother or to prevail on myself, to
disuse the traffic or the potation of brandy, but
perhaps a pledge of total abstinence might effec-
tually restrain us.   The candidate my party
votes for is not to be trusted with a dollar, but
he will be honest in the Senate, for we can
bring public opinion to bear on him.   Thus
concert was the specific in all cases.   But concert is neither better nor worse, neither more
nor less potent than individual force.   All the
men in the world cannot make a statue walk
and speak, cannot make a drop of blood, or a
blade of grass, any more than one man can.
But let there be one man, let there be truth in
two men, in ten men, then is concert for the first
time possible, because the force which moves

the world is a new quality, and can never be
furnished by adding whatever quantities of a
different kind.   What is the use of the concert
of the false and the disunited?   There can be
no concert in two, where there is no concert in
one.   When the individual is not *individual*, but
is dual; when his thoughts look one way, and
his actions another; when his faith is traversed
by his habits; when his will, enlightened by
reason, is warped by his sense; when with one
hand he rows, and with the other backs water,
what concert can be?

I do not wonder at the interest these projects
inspire.   The world is awaking to the idea of
union, and these experiments show what it is
thinking of.   It is and will be magic.   Men will
live and communicate, and plough, and reap,
and govern, as by added ethereal power, when
once they are united; as in a celebrated experiment, by expiration and respiration exactly together, four persons lift a heavy man from the
ground by the little finger only, and without
sense of weight.   But this union must be inward,
and not one of covenants, and is to be reached
by a reverse of the methods they use.   The
union is only perfect, when all the uniters are

isolated.   It is the union of friends who live in
different streets or towns.   Each man, if he attempts to join himself to others, is on all sides
cramped and diminished of his proportion ; and
the stricter the union, the smaller and the more
pitiful he is.   But leave him alone, to recognize
in every hour and place the secret soul, he will
go up and down doing the works of a true
member, and, to the astonishment of all, the
work will be done with concert, though no man
spoke.   Government will be adamantine without any governor.   The union must be ideal in
actual individualism.

I pass to the indication in some particulars
of that faith in man, which the heart is preaching to us in these days, and which engages the
more regard, from the consideration, that the
speculations of one generation are the history
of the next following.

In alluding just now to our system of education, I spoke of the deadness of its details.
But it is open to graver criticism than the palsy
of its members : it is a system of despair.   The
disease with which the human mind now labors,
is want of faith.   Men do not believe in a
power of education.   We do not think we can

speak to divine sentiments in man, and we do
not try. We renounce all high aims. We believe that the defects of so many perverse and
so many frivolous people, who make up society,
are organic, and society is a hospital of incura-
bles. A man of good sense but of little faith,
whose compassion seemed to lead him to church
as often as he went there, said to me ; " that he
liked to have concerts, and fairs, and churches,
and other public amusements go on." I am
afraid the remark is too honest, and comes from
the same origin as the maxim of the tyrant, "If
you would rule the world quietly, you must
keep it amused." I notice too, that the ground
on which eminent public servants urge the
claims of popular education is fear : ' This
country is filling up with thousands and millions
of voters, and you must educate them to keep
them from our throats.' We do not believe
that any education, any system of philosophy,
any influence of genius, will ever give depth of
insight to a superficial mind. Having settled
ourselves into this infidelity, our skill is expended to procure alleviations, diversion, opi-
ates. We adorn the victim with manual skill,
his tongue with languages, his body with in-
44

offensive and comely manners. So have we cunningly hid the tragedy of limitation and inner death we cannot avert. Is it strange that society should be devoured by a secret melancholy, which breaks through all its smiles, and all its gayety and games?

But even one step farther our infidelity has gone. It appears that some doubt is felt by good and wise men, whether really the happiness and probity of men is increased by the culture of the mind in those disciplines to which we give the name of education. Unhappily, too, the doubt comes from scholars, from persons who have tried these methods. In their experience, the scholar was not raised by the sacred thoughts amongst which he dwelt, but used them to selfish ends. He was a profane person, and became a showman, turning his gifts to a marketable use, and not to his own sustenance and growth. It was found that the intellect could be independently developed, that is, in separation from the man, as any single organ can be invigorated, and the result was monstrous. A canine appetite for knowledge was generated, which must still be fed, but was never satisfied, and this knowledge not being directed on action, never took the character of substantial, humane truth, blessing those whom it entered. It gave the scholar certain powers of expression, the power of speech, the power of poetry, of literary art, but it did not bring him to peace, or to beneficence.

When the literary class betray a destitution of faith, it is not strange that society should be disheartened and sensualized by unbelief. What remedy? Life must be lived on a higher plane. We must go up to a higher platform, to which we are always invited to ascend; there, the whole aspect of things changes. I resist the skepticism of our education, and of our educated men. I do not believe that the differences of opinion and character in men are organic. I do not recognize, beside the class of the good and the wise, a permanent class of skeptics, or a class of conservatives, or of malignants, or of materialists. I do not believe in two classes. You remember the story of the poor woman who importuned King Philip of Macedon to grant her justice, which Philip refused: the woman exclaimed, " I appeal ": the king, astonished, asked to whom she appealed:

the woman replied, "from Philip drunk to Philip
sober." The text will suit me very well. I believe not in two classes of men, but in man in
two moods, in Philip drunk and Philip sober.
I think, according to the good-hearted word of
Plato, "Unwillingly the soul is deprived of
truth." Iron conservative, miser, or thief, no
man is, but by a supposed necessity, which he
tolerates by shortness or torpidity of sight.
The soul lets no man go without some visita-
tions and holy-days of a diviner presence. It
would be easy to show, by a narrow scanning
of any man's biography, that we are not so
wedded to our paltry performances of every
kind, but that every man has at intervals the
grace to scorn his performances, in comparing
them with his belief of what he should do, that
he puts himself on the side of his enemies,
listening gladly to what they say of him, and
accusing himself of the same things.

What is it men love in Genius, but its infi-
nite hope, which degrades all it has done?
Genius counts all its miracles poor and short.
Its own idea it never executed. The Iliad, the
Hamlet, the Doric column, the Roman arch,
the Gothic minster, the German anthem, when

they are ended, the master casts behind him. How sinks the song in the waves of melody which the universe pours over his soul! Before that gracious Infinite, out of which he drew these few strokes, how mean they look, though the praises of the world attend them. From the triumphs of his art, he turns with desire to this greater defeat. Let those admire who will. With silent joy he sees himself to be capable of a beauty that eclipses all which his hands have done, all which human hands have ever done.

Well, we are all the children of genius, the children of virtue,—and feel their inspirations in our happier hours. Is not every man sometimes a radical in politics? Men are conservatives when they are least vigorous, or when they are most luxurious. They are conservatives after dinner, or before taking their rest; when they are sick, or aged: in the morning, or when their intellect or their conscience have been aroused, when they hear music, or when they read poetry, they are radicals. In the circle of the rankest tories that could be collected in England, Old or New, let a powerful and stimulating intellect, a man of great heart

and mind, act on them, and very quickly these
frozen conservators will yield to the friendly
influence, these hopeless will begin to hope,
these haters will begin to love, these immovable
statues will begin to spin and revolve. I cannot help recalling the fine anecdote which
Warton relates of Bishop Berkeley, when he
was preparing to leave England, with his plan
of planting the gospel among the American
savages. " Lord Bathurst told me, that the
members of the Scriblerus club, being met at
his house at dinner, they agreed to rally Berkeley, who was also his guest, on his scheme at
Bermudas. Berkeley, having listened to the
many lively things they had to say, begged to
be heard in his turn, and displayed his plan
with such an astonishing and animating force
of eloquence and enthusiasm, that they were
struck dumb, and, after some pause, rose up all
together with earnestness, exclaiming, ' Let us
set out with him immediately.' " Men in all
ways are better than they seem. They like
flattery for the moment, but they know the
truth for their own. It is a foolish cowardice
which keeps us from trusting them, and speaking to them rude truth. They resent your

honesty for an instant, they will thank you for
it always. What is it we heartly wish of each
other? Is it to be pleased and flattered? No,
but to be convicted and exposed, to be shamed
out of our nonsense of all kinds, and made men
of, instead of ghosts and phantoms. We are
weary of gliding ghostlike through the world,
which is itself so slight and unreal. We crave
a sense of reality, though it come in strokes of
pain. I explain so,—by this manlike love of
truth,—those excesses and errors into which
souls of great vigor, but not equal insight, often
fall. They feel the poverty at the bottom of all
the seeming affluence of the world. They
know the speed with which they come straight
through the thin masquerade, and conceive a
disgust at the indigence of nature: Rousseau,
Mirabeau, Charles Fox, Napoleon, Byron,—
and I could easily add names nearer home, of
raging riders, who drive their steeds so hard,
in the violence of living to forget its illusion:
they would know the worst, and tread the
floors of hell. The heroes of ancient and
modern fame, Cimon, Themistocles, Alcibi-
ades, Alexander, Cæsar, have treated life and
fortune as a game to be well and skilfully

played, but the stake not to be so valued, but that any time, it could be held as a trifle light as air, and thrown up. Cæsar, just before the battle of Pharsalia, discourses with the Egyptian priest, concerning the fountains of the Nile, and offers to quit the army, the empire, and Cleopatra, if he will show him those mysterious sources.

The same magnanimity shows itself in our social relations, in the preference, namely, which each man gives to the society of superiors over that of his equals. All that a man has, will he give for right relations with his mates. All that he has, will he give for an erect demeanor in every company and on each occasion. He aims at such things as his neighbors prize, and gives his days and nights, his talents and his heart, to strike a good stroke, to acquit himself in all men's sight as a man. The consideration of an eminent citizen, of a noted merchant, of a man of mark in his profession; naval and military honor, a general's commission, a marshal's baton, a ducal coronet, the laurel of poets, and, anyhow procured, the acknowledgment of eminent merit, have this lustre for each candidate, that they enable him to walk erect and

unashamed, in the presence of some persons,
before whom he felt himself inferior.   Having
raised himself to this rank, having established
his equality with class after class, of those with
whom he would live well, he still finds certain
others, before whom he cannot possess himself, because they have somewhat fairer, somewhat grander, somewhat purer, which extorts
homage of him.   Is his ambition pure? then,
will his laurels and his possessions seem worthless: instead of avoiding these men who make
his fine gold dim, he will cast all behind him,
and seek their society only, woo and embrace
this his humiliation and mortification, until he
shall know why his eye sinks, his voice is
husky, and his brilliant talents are paralyzed
in this presence.   He is sure that the soul which
gives the lie to all things, will tell none.   His
constitution will not mislead him.   If it cannot
carry itself as it ought, high and unmatchable
in the presence of any man, if the secret oracles
whose whisper makes the sweetness and dignity
of his life, do here withdraw and accompany
him no longer, it is time to undervalue what he
has valued, to dispossess himself of what he has
acquired, and with Cæsar to take in his hand

the army, the empire, and Cleopatra, and say, 'All these will I relinquish, if you will show me the fountains of the Nile.' Dear to us are those who love us, the swift moments we spend with them are a compensation for a great deal of misery; they enlarge our life;—but dearer are those who reject us as unworthy, for they add another life: they build a heaven before us, whereof we had not dreamed, and thereby supply to us new powers out of the recesses of the spirit, and urge us to new and unattempted performances.

As every man at heart wishes the best and not inferior society, wishes to be convicted of his error, and to come to himself, so he wishes that the same healing should not stop in his thought, but should penetrate his will or active power. The selfish man suffers more from his selfishness, than he from whom that selfishness withholds some important benefit. What he most wishes is to be lifted to some higher platform, that he may see beyond his present fear the transalpine good, so that his fear, his coldness, his custom may be broken up like fragments of ice, melted and carried away in the great stream of good will. Do you ask my aid?

I also wish to be a benefactor. I wish more to be a benefactor and servant, than you wish to be served by me, and surely the greatest good fortune that could befall me, is precisely to be so moved by you that I should say, ' Take me and all mine, and use me and mine freely to your ends'! for, I could not say it, otherwise than because a great enlargement had come to my heart and mind, which made me superior to my fortunes. Here we are paralyzed with fear ; we hold on to our little properties, house and land, office and money, for the bread which they have in our experience yielded us, although we confess, that our being does not flow through them. We desire to be made great, we desire to be touched with that fire which shall command this ice to stream, and make our existence a benefit. If therefore we start objections to your project, O friend of the slave, or friend of the poor, or of the race, understand well, that it is because we wish to drive you to drive us into your measures. We wish to hear ourselves confuted. We are haunted with a belief that you have a secret, which it would highliest advantage us to learn, and we would force you to impart it to us, though it should bring us to prison, or to worse extremity.

Nothing shall warp me from the belief, that every man is a lover of truth. There is no pure lie, no pure malignity in nature. The entertainment of the proposition of depravity is the last profligacy and profanation. There is no skepticism, no atheism but that. Could it be received into common belief, suicide would unpeople the planet. It has had a name to live in some dogmatic theology, but each man's innocence and his real liking of his neighbor, have kept it a dead letter. I remember standing at the polls one day, when the anger of the political contest gave a certain grimness to the faces of the independent electors, and a good man at my side looking on the people, remarked, " I am satisfied that the largest part of these men, on either side, mean to vote right." I suppose, considerate observers looking at the masses of men, in their blameless, and in their equivocal actions, will assent, that in spite of selfishness and frivolity, the general purpose in the great number of persons is fidelity. The reason why any one refuses his assent to your opinion, or his aid to your benevolent design, is in you : he refuses to accept you as a bringer of truth, because, though you think you have it, he feels that you have it not. You have not given him the authentic sign.

If it were worth while to run into details this general doctrine of the latent but ever soliciting Spirit, it would be easy to adduce illustration in particulars of a man's equality to the church, of his equality to the state, and of his equality to every other man. It is yet in all men's memory, that, a few years ago, the liberal churches complained, that the Calvinistic church denied to them the name of Christian. I think the complaint was confession : a religious church would not complain. A religious man like Behmen, Fox, or Swedenborg, is not irritated by wanting the sanction of the church, but the church feels the accusation of his presence and belief.

It only needs, that a just man should walk in our streets, to make it appear how pitiful and inartificial a contrivance is our legislation. The man whose part is taken, and who does not wait for society in anything, has a power which society cannot choose but feel. The familiar experiment, called the hydrostatic paradox, in which a capillary column of water balances the ocean, is a symbol of the relation of one man to the whole family of men.   The wise Dandini, on hearing the lives of Socrates, Pythagoras, and Diogenes read, "judged them to be great men every way, excepting, that they were too much subjected to the reverence of the laws, which to second and authorize, true virtue must abate very much of its original vigor."

And as a man is equal to the church, and equal to the state, so he is equal to every other man.   The disparities of power in men are superficial; and all frank and searching conversation, in which a man lays himself open to his brother, apprizes each of their radical unity. When two persons sit and converse in a thoroughly good understanding, the remark is sure to be made, See how we have disputed about words!   Let a clear, apprehensive mind, such as every man knows among his friends, converse with the most commanding poetic genius, I think, it would appear that there was no inequality such as men fancy between them; that a perfect understanding, a like receiving, a like perceiving, abolished differences, and the poet would confess, that his creative imagination gave him no deep advantage, but only the superficial one, that he could express himself, and the other could not; that his advantage was a knack, which might impose on indolent men, but could not impose on lovers of truth ; for they know the tax of talent, or, what a price of greatness the power of expression too often pays. I believe it is the conviction of the purest men, that the net amount of man and man does not much vary. Each is incomparably superior to his companion in some faculty. His want of skill in other directions, has added to his fitness for his own work. Each seems to have some compensation yielded to him by his infirmity, and every hindrance operates as a concentration of his force.

These and the like experiences intimate, that man stands in strict connexion with a higher fact never yet manifested. There is power over and behind us, and we are the channels of its communications. We seek to say thus and so, and over our head some spirit sits, which contradicts what we say. We would persuade our fellow to this or that ; another self within our eyes dissuades him. That which we keep back, this reveals. In vain we compose our faces and our words; it holds uncontrollable communication with the enemy, and he answers

civilly to us, but believes the spirit. We ex-
claim, ' There's a traitor in the house!' but at
last it appears that he is the true man, and I am
the traitor. This open channel to the highest
life is the first and last reality, so subtle, so
quiet, yet so tenacious, that although I have
never expressed the truth, and although I have
never heard the expression of it from any other,
I know that the whole truth is here for me.
What if I cannot answer your questions? I
am not pained that I cannot frame a reply to
the question, What is the operation we call
Providence? There lies the unspoken thing,
present, omnipresent. Every time we converse,
we seek to translate it into speech, but whether
we hit, or whether we miss, we have the fact.
Every discourse is an approximate answer: but
it is of small consequence, that we do not get
it into verbs and nouns, whilst it abides for con-
templation forever.

If the auguries of the prophesying heart shall
make themselves good in time, the man who
shall be born, whose advent men and events
prepare and foreshow, is one who shall enjoy
his connexion with a higher life, with the man
within man; shall destroy distrust by his trust,

shall use his native but forgotten methods, shall not take counsel of flesh and blood, but shall rely on the Law alive and beautiful, which works over our heads and under our feet.   Pitiless, it avails itself of our success, when we obey it, and of our ruin, when we contravene it.   Men are all secret believers in it, else, the word justice would have no meaning : they believe that the best is the true ; that right is done at last ; or chaos would come.   It rewards actions after their nature, and not after the design of the agent.   ' Work,' it saith to man, ' in every hour, paid or unpaid, see only that thou work, and thou canst not escape the reward : whether thy work be fine or coarse, planting corn, or writing epics, so only it be honest work, done to thine own approbation, it shall earn a reward to the senses as well as to the thought : no matter, how often defeated, you are born to victory. The reward of a thing well done, is to have done it.'

As soon as a man is wonted to look beyond surfaces, and to see how this high will prevails without an exception or an interval, he settles himself into serenity.   He can already rely on the laws of gravity, that every stone will fall

45

where it is due ; the good globe is faithful, and carries us securely through the celestial spaces, anxious or resigned : we need not interfere to help it on, and he will learn, one day, the mild lesson they teach, that our own orbit is all our task, and we need not assist the administration of the universe. Do not be so impatient to set the town right concerning the unfounded pretensions and the false reputation of certain men of standing. They are laboring harder to set the town right concerning themselves, and will certainly succeed. Suppress for a few days your criticism on the insufficiency ·of this or that teacher or experimenter, and he will have demonstrated his insufficiency to all men's eyes. In like manner, let a man fall into the divine circuits, and he is enlarged. Obedience to his genius is the only liberating influence. We wish to escape from subjection, and a sense of inferiority, —and we make self-denying ordinances, we drink water, we eat grass, we refuse the laws, we go to jail : it is all in vain ; only by obedience to his genius ; only by the freest activity in the way constitutional to him, does an angel seem to arise before a man, and lead him by the hand out of all the wards of the prison.

That which befits us, embosomed in beauty and wonder as we are, is cheerfulness and courage, and the endeavor to realize our aspirations. The life of man is the true romance, which, when it is valiantly conducted, will yield the imagination a higher joy than any fiction. All around us, what powers are wrapped up under the coarse mattings of custom, and all wonder prevented. It is so wonderful to our neurologists that a man can see without his eyes, that it does not occur to them, that it is just as wonderful, that he should see with them; and that is ever the difference between the wise and the unwise: the latter wonders at what is unusual, the wise man wonders at the usual. Shall not the heart which has received so much, trust the Power by which it lives? May it not quit other leadings, and listen to the Soul that has guided it so gently, and taught it so much, secure that the future will be worthy of the past?